GEORGES RODENBACH
POEMS

Rodenbach smoking
Photo by Nadar, 1895

Georges Rodenbach
POEMS

Selected, translated & introduced by
WILL STONE

Guest edited by
OLIVIA HANKS

Arc
PUBLICATIONS
2017

Published by Arc Publications,
Nanholme Mill, Shaw Wood Road
Todmorden OL14 6DA, UK
www.arcpublications.co.uk

Copyright © Estate of Georges Rodenbach, 2017
Translation copyright © Will Stone, 2017
Introduction copyright © Will Stone, 2017
Copyright in the present edition © Arc Publications, 2017

Design by Tony Ward
Printed in Great Britain by
TJ International, Padstow, Cornwall

978 1904614 64 7 (pbk)
978 1906570 07 1 (hbk)
978 1910345 12 2 (ebook)

Cover photo: Nadar, 1895

ACKNOWLEDGEMENTS

Arc Publications and the translator wish to express their thanks to the Ministère de la Communauté française – Bruxelles and L'Académie royale de langue et de littérature françaises de Belgique for their generous support and patience in the realization of this project. The publishers would also like to thank the Archives et Musée de la littérature – Bibliothèque Royale, Bruxelles, for allowing them to reproduce the photographs on the cover and on pp. 2, 8, 12, 15 & 108.

This book is in copyright. Subject to statutory exception and to provision of relevant collective licensing agreements, no reproduction of any part of this book may take place without the written permission of Arc Publications.

ARTS COUNCIL ENGLAND
LOTTERY FUNDED

'Arc Classics' Translation Series –
New Translations of Great Poets of the Past
Series Editor: Jean Boase-Beier

Translator's Acknowledgements

These translations constitute the first full-length collection of Rodenbach's poetry to be published in the English language. I would like to express my gratitude to a number of bodies, both in the UK and on the continent, for their financial support for the labours of translation.

Firstly, my gratitude goes to The Society of Authors in London, Arts Council England (East) and the Centre National du Livre (CNL) in Paris. Also to Le Centre International des Traducteurs Littéraires (CITL) in Arles for providing a residency to work on the translation and especially to Le Collège Européen des Traducteurs Littéraires de Seneffe in Belgium. I would like to personally thank its president Jacques de Decker and director Françoise Wuilmart, whose faith, generosity and continued hospitality down the years allowed me to carry out the necessary work over a number of residencies.

I should also like to thank Paul Etienne Kisters in the Archives et Musée de la Littérature for his time and trouble in tracking down certain photographs and likewise the courteous staff of the Cabinet des Estampes in the Bibliothèque Royal de Belgique for their expert guidance. I am grateful, too, for the assistance given by Rodenbach scholar Joël Goffin and helpful advice from Silvie Philippart de Foy in the 'Promotion des Lettres' department in Le Ministère de la Communauté Française.

I also express sincere thanks to bookseller Anette Van de Wiele in Bruges for her long-standing friendship and her expertise in tracking down relevant books and texts, to my Editor at Arc, Professor Jean Boase-Beier for her patience and sound advice, and to Olivia Hanks for her valuable editorial contribution. I would like to thank poets Paul Stubbs and Blandine Longre of Black Herald Press in Paris for publishing some of these translations in their excellent journal. Also thank you to poets Richie McCaffrey in Ghent and Stephen Romer in Tours for their personal interest in this collection and their continued friendship. Finally I would like to thank Emma Mountcastle in Devon for her crucial supportive presence behind my literary endeavours and my parents for the continuing gift of their humanity.

Will Stone

Contents

Introduction / 9

de *La Jeunesse Blanche* / from *The White Youth*
24 / Dimanches • Sundays / 25
26 / Seul • Alone / 27
28 / Vieux Quais • Old Quays / 29
32 / Nocturne • Nocturne / 33
34 / Départ • Departure / 35
36 / Solitude • Solitude / 37
38 / La Passion • The Passion / 39

de *Le Règne du Silence* / from *The Reign of Silence*
40 / La vie des chambres (IV, VI, • The Life of Rooms (IV, VI, VIII,
   VIII, XIII, XV)   XIII, XV) / 41
50 / Le coeur de l'eau (X-XII) • The Water's Heart (X-XII) / 51
56 / Paysages de ville (IV, VI, XII, XIV) • Landscapes of Towns (IV, VI, XII, XIV) / 57
64 / Cloches de Dimanche (II, V, XII) • Sunday Bells (II, V, XII) / 65
70 / Au fil de l'âme (I, IX) • On the Soul's Flow (I, IX) / 71
74 / Du silence (I, VII, XIV, XXI-XXV) • Of Silence (I, VII, XIV, XXI-XXV) / 75

de *Les Vies Encloses* / from *The Enclosed Lives*
84 / Aquarium Mental (I, IX) • Mental Aquarium (I, IX) / 85
88 / Le soir dans les vitres (XI) • Evening in the Windows (XI) / 89
90 / Les lignes de la main (I) • The Lines of the Hand (I) / 91
92 / Les malades aux fenêtres (IV, XII, XIII) • Invalids at the Windows (IV, XII, XIII) / 93

de *Plusieurs Poèmes* / from *Several Poems*
98 / Pour la gloire de Mallarmé • For the Glory of Mallarmé / 99

de *Le Miroir du Ciel Natal* / from *The Mirror of the Native Sky*
100 / Les femmes en mantes (extrait) • The Women in Mantles / 101
102 / Les réverbères (V-VI) • The Street Lamps (V-VI) / 103
106 / Les cygnes (VI) • The Swans (VI) / 107

Biographical Notes / 109

Old Bruges (date unknown)

INTRODUCTION

'The word is time, silence eternity...'
MAETERLINCK

The poetic of silence is, with Rodenbach, an 'abstraction' by which the most concrete sensual notation escapes its conventional context to integrate with a subtle network of images, sometimes unexpected but all gathered in the single converging beam of the imaginary. And here then is one of Rodenbach's great merits, to have grasped and profited poetically from that superior unity of the imaginary beyond the prosaic syntax of the 'real'.
PATRICK LAUDE

There is an intriguing work of art hanging in the Musée d'Orsay to which visitors are customarily attracted. It is a portrait of a man half-framed by an open window, with an ancient Flemish town in the background akin to those one sees in the canvases of the Flemish Primitives, a town one might guess is Bruges by the distinctive medieval canal bridge, the lofty tower and the leaded panes of Venetian glass in the half-open window. The pastel gives the image a dreamy, indistinct quality and one is drawn into the seductive, yet vaguely unsettling, territory of reverie or mild hallucination. The man's face is sickly and wan as if he has spent too long inside, his lips are a vague, watery pink, his eyes languid, the lids barely able to resist closing, his smoke puff of moustache and light hair a washed-out sandy shade. He is a spectral figure drifting across the canal's greenish-black waters, his dark jacket blending naturally with its opaque surface, suggesting an area of confusion where dream and reality converge. Lucien Lèvy Dhurmer, a friend of Georges Rodenbach's, made his famous pastel of the poet around 1895, a few years after the publication of *Bruges-la-Morte*, the novel which made the writer's name. Although Rodenbach never lived in Bruges, he will forever be associated with the proverbial 'Venice of the North' through his extraordinary evocations of its decaying late nineteenth-century atmosphere. Published in Paris in 1892, this story of a lonely widower's fetishist designs on a common actress takes place within a mesmerising poetic distillation of Bruges' 'ville morte' (dead town) atmosphere. The novel particularly appealed to the romantic imagination of a generation of erudite Parisians yearning for escape into myth and mysticism, so much so that it outsold all other novels in France that year and gave rise to a new kind of pilgrimage to the decaying northern canal town. Yet the writer of this novel was a poet who had been writing poems on this same subject over the years preceding its appearance. Indeed, only the year before he had published a volume of poetry entitled *The Reign of Silence* (1891) which prefigured much of the poetic prose contained in *Bruges-la-Morte*. It is this collection of poetry, considered to be the core of Rodenbach's poetic vision, that forms the axis of the present volume. In terms of Bruges, *The Reign of Silence* and the two collections which followed, *The Enclosed Lives* (1896) and *The Mirror of the Native Sky* (1898) are the culmination of an imaginative treatment of Bruges as a supernatural landscape, where what is seemingly dead speaks, where the worn-away stone, even the grass and moss growing up through the cobblestones, have a voice detected only by those who are endowed with the sensibility to receive the true soul of the town. It is this treatment of Bruges as a poetic vehicle for a mood, one of supreme melancholy, which forms the backbone of not only these poems but Rodenbach's entire oeuvre.

* * *

Georges Rodenbach was born in Tournai in 1855, the same year as the poet Emile Verhaeren, with whom he would share the benches of the College Saint Barbe in Ghent until 1875, then, like Verhaeren, go on to study – and, in Rodenbach's case, practise – law. Flemish born and bred, he chose, like Verhaeren and Maeterlinck, to write in French, the language of the dominant political and intellectual culture, and as a consequence, along with his two compatriots, was regarded by a vociferous portion of his countrymen as a traitor to his native roots and scornfully dubbed 'fransquillon'. According to his biographer Pierre Maes, Rodenbach came from ancient Germanic stock, and his ancestors, including doctors, historians and men of science, were all in one way or another talented writers. Maes speculates that the grafting of these Germanic roots onto the Flemish culture created, in Rodenbach, "a poetic sensibility refined to the extreme, the last gift from nature achieving the perfect representation of a family predestined for art", and one might argue that his predilection for mysticism, melancholia and profound contemplation were inherited characteristics.

Rodenbach's first literary steps were tentative and taken on home ground; a poem was published in a Brussels magazine and he attended a literary salon in Ghent with his trusted friend Verhaeren. At this time, the early 1880s, he was observed by the novelist Camille Lemonnier who described him in his book *Belgian Life* in a wholly different way to that of a brooding and anxiety-torn loner: "So then Rodenbach, most cordial, with a youthful carefree impetuosity, a voice clear as brass! No laugh was fuller than his; he was all gaiety, candour, conviction. A vital blood, that in warmer moments caused that face recalling a young ram with pale yellowish brown eyes to blush beneath the fair astrakhan hair. He shone above all at literary readings, spoke in images, profligate, rich and fluent, lingering at the ends of sentences, one hand raised in a priestly gesture." In order to complete his studies, Rodenbach was dispatched to Paris in 1878 and was almost immediately drawn into the literary ferment, becoming close to a new group of literati containing a number of distinguished French poets and writers of the day known as the 'Hydropathes', a kind of predecessor to the decadents and symbolists. In Paris he came into contact with most of the great and lesser figures of the symbolist epoch, J. K. Huysmans, Alphonse Daudet, Theodore de Banville, Catulle Mendès, François Coppée, Maurice Barrès and most importantly Edmond de Goncourt and Stephane Mallarmé. He also met Victor Hugo and an ageing Verlaine. He contributed articles to Parisian magazines such as *La Plume* and *La Paix*. Returning to Brussels he entered the legal profession, making a name for himself as a smooth legal operator, one of his most successful coups being the acquittal of Max Waller, founder of La Jeune Belgique (Young Belgium) literary group. Rodenbach fought against the petty wrangles and depressing officialdom of the literary establishment, winning friends and admirers in the new radical movements springing up in the early 1880s; known for his tact, diplomacy, subtlety and restraint, Rodenbach became an immensely popular figure in both Brussels and Paris.

In 1881, along with Emile Verhaeren, Max Elskamp, Maurice Maeterlinck and others, Rodenbach was caught up in the Belgian literary revival initially centred around the revolutionary group La Jeune Belgique and was a central figure as new movements and magazines with different agendas fought for prominence in Brussels. Eventually, however, he became disillusioned with the political cut and thrust and decided to move permanently to Paris. He was the first of his contemporaries to make this move, but others followed, including Verhaeren a decade later. Safely installed in Paris, Rodenbach contributed his weekly 'Parisian Letters' to the *Journal de Bruxelles* as well as working as correspondent for *Le Figaro*. Rodenbach became one of the faithful at 'les mardis' (meetings which took place on a Tuesday) in Mallarmé's house in the Rue de Rome. He also frequented the salon of Madame Daudet and the 'grenier' in Auteuil, where Edmond de Goncourt received his friends. In 1888 he married Anna-Maria Urbain who gave birth to a son in 1892, the same year as *Bruges-la-Morte* appeared.

Rodenbach never lived in Bruges but he made repeated prolonged visits there; one rare picture (date unknown) shows him in a straw hat sitting with a couple of friends on simple wooden chairs in the long grass of the meadow of the béguinage, casually observing the daily customs of the béguines. He always returned to Paris, however, where his rarefied poetic prose with its romantic leanings and all-pervasive melancholia continued to strike a chord with the reading classes of Paris, seeing his gradual eclipse from being just another dandified *fin-de-siècle* poet to the authentic voice of a mystical Bruges. Having grown up in an area studded with so called 'dead towns' (once prosperous provincial centres, criss-crossed by canals, now fallen into disuse and decay), he was profoundly affected by the mournful atmosphere which saturated these ghost towns. In his essay *The Death Agonies of Towns* (1897) – primarily about Bruges, though Ypres, Furnes, Courtrai and others are cited – he attempts to articulate the atmosphere of isolation and abandonment of those 'melancholic widows of medieval communes', explaining that the death of Bruges was caused by the drying up of the Zwijn Canal in 1475 and the permanent retreat of the North Sea: "Bruges, now at some distance from that mighty breast of the ocean which had nourished her children, began to bleed dry and for long centuries lay in the shadow of death." His depiction of Bruges as a corpse is maintained through a plethora of references: huddled nuns the "servants of her death throes", their steps dying away "like a death knell", the once prosperous town now "shivering in the bareness of its stones". He describes the silence of these dead towns – a silence which both protects and infects and ultimately dominates, but which in its turn can be wounded by intruding voices – and the ever-present sound of bells, the myriad carillons of Bruges: "And it is for her funeral that a bell in the distance chimes! Now others are ringing out, but so vague, so ponderous, like a rain of dark flowers, like the dust of cold ashes from these urns which sway gently from the distant towers." Like a painter searching his palette for the right mix, he describes the famous belfry of Bruges as "the harsh belfry, the colour of wine lees, of rust, of blood and of a waning sun…" while the windows of ancient dwellings are "of a mournful bluish-green" and the façades "fade in nuances of yellowed pallor, washed out greens, antiquated pinks, that sing softly the silent melody of faded hues." Even the windmills on the edge of town are agents of melancholia, their sails seeming "to be grinding down a patch of sky."

Unlike his later works of the 1990s, Rodenbach's early poems tend to be a mixture of doomed love entanglements, romantic longing, rhetorical eulogies over the graves of his siblings and a patchwork of quasi-evangelic sentiments, although the repetitive qualities which characterise his mature output are already in evidence. In his poetry of the 1880s, the Parnassian influence slowly gives way to symbolism – although Rodenbach, unlike Verhaeren, maintains a formal metered structure, believing that metered verse is most sympathetic to the symbolist lyric, and seeing any departure from it as a betrayal of tradition. In his aversion to progress and his hankering after the past lies proof that Rodenbach remains both spiritually and practically a nineteenth-century poet rather than one who straddles the nineteenth and twentieth centuries like Verhaeren. His premature death in 1898, aged only 43, seems to underscore this still further. To Mallarmé's famous proclamation "To name an object is to suppress three quarters of a poem's pleasure, which should be divined little by little. To suggest, that is the dream", Rodenbach responds: "Symbolist poetry is the dream, nuances the art of travel within the clouds which tame reflections, where the real is only a point of departure and the paper itself, a fragile white certainty, from where one ascends into the ethereal space of mystery…"

It could be said that Rodenbach, with his passion for his native land's rich history and artistic heritage, sought through his poetry to unite Belgian symbolism with its French counterpart. There were, however, those such as Edmond Picard who somewhat cynically reproached Rodenbach for creating a Flanders of his imagination which would naturally appeal to Parisian tastes. But Rodenbach had clearly stated his need to distance himself physically from the provincial, for only by so doing could its memory be enhanced through the nostalgic imagination: "It's only after having relinquished our native Flanders, our Flanders of childhood and adolescence to settle definitively in Paris, that we are able to write poetry and prose as recollection... the Flanders that we have recreated and revived through the deception of art." The criticisms directed at him, particularly by the Flemish nationalists following the success of *Bruges-la-Morte*, for his depiction of a town they were trying to revive commercially as "morte" weighed heavily on him. For his Flemish critics, this Gallic dandy, who persisted in opposing change and modernity by his unrealistic harking back to the past, who wanted to keep Bruges locked in silence and immutability, was a serious threat to their ambitions. When a sculpture in memory of Rodenbach by Georges Minne was presented to Bruges in 1899, it was refused following pressure by a group of townspeople led by local Flemish poet Guido Gezelle; four years later, it was erected near the béguinage in Ghent, where it still resides to this day.

Rodenbach at home in Paris

Notwithstanding the criticism from inside his own country, Rodenbach's influence in the literary circles of Paris grew steadily from the early 1890s. Cultivating an uncompromising aesthetic which went hand-in-hand with his dandyism, he became one of the most cherished members of Mallarmé's elite circle. He was at the height of his career when the chest complaint that had dogged him for some years suddenly worsened and, aged only 43, he died in the final days of 1898, the same year in which both Mallarmé and the painter Gustave Moreau died. Rodenbach was buried in Père Lachaise cemetery in a distinctive tomb now known as 'l'homme à la rose'. After his death, Rodenbach's work continued to impress and influence fellow writers and also the composer Erich Korngold, who based his opera *Die tote Stadt* (1920) on *Bruges-la-Morte*. Apart from Proust, perhaps the most significant writer to champion Rodenbach's poetry was Rilke, who was probably directed towards Rodenbach and Bruges by his friend Verhaeren, when resident in Paris from 1902. Rilke's travels to Bruges by way of medieval Furnes (now Veurne) were possibly also the result of encouragement from a young Stefan Zweig, who had made the trip a few years earlier, likewise on Verhaeren's advice. Rilke's new poems of 1907-8 show the probable influence of Rodenbach in their tendency to reveal the interior life of objects; certainly the delicacy and refinement of Rodenbach's poetic voice could hardly have found a more discerning and understanding listener than Rilke.

* * *

Rodenbach's poetry collections tend to be long, and in some cases repetitious, and consequently there is a vast body of work to choose from. For this volume, I have chosen poems that both underpin and extend the prose poetry contained in *Bruges-la-Morte* and further writings concerned with Bruges, selecting them from four of the poet's major collections: *The White Youth* (1886), *The Reign of Silence* (1891) *The Enclosed Lives* (1896) and *The Mirror of the Native Sky* (1898).

Rodenbach's first collections were published initially as chapbooks. His poetic debut was in 1877 with *Le Foyer et les champs*, (The Home and the Fields) followed by *Les Tristesses* (The Sorrows, 1879), *La Mer Elegante* (The Elegant Sea, 1881) and *L'Hiver Mondain* (Urbane Winter, 1884). These early collections, however, were later rejected by their author as having been published prematurely, with Rodenbach at pains to emphasise that his vision proper began with *The White Youth*, written in 1884-5 and published by Lemerre in Paris in 1886. This was a book that Pierre Maes and others saw as representing the transition from the rigid old Parnassian school to the realm of symbolism and marks the point at which Rodenbach committed himself to the construction of a mythical Flanders and the association of the 'dead city' with his interior life. The colour white is chosen here for what can be seen as a symbolic disappearance of colour, something close to silence, the page on which life shall appear and the neutral background required for art to begin. Rodenbach continues to employ colour symbolically, particularly white, throughout his oeuvre – we observe it as swans, candles, altar clothes, lilies and the robes of the first communicants – and by the time of *The Mirror of the Native Sky*, almost everything is immersed in this white, even the music of the bells. With *The White Youth*, Rodenbach begins his long walk back to the past, in poems suffused with the woody aroma of old incense and the sound of pious footfalls in the dark recesses of the ambulatory. Schopenhauer presides as chief embalmer; other players are a throng of French poets headed by Verlaine and Baudelaire. The latter's voice is perhaps heard most forcefully, especially in poems such as 'Alone', 'Departure' and 'Solitude', which also sit comfortably alongside the Verhaeren of *Les Soirs* (The Evenings) from the *Trilogie Noire* which appeared only a year later. The real importance of the poems in *The White Youth* as compared to the somewhat biographical verses which preceded them is the link between the distance of memory and reality. The distancing of Flanders allows for the growth of poetry in the very gap that is left; the analogy can develop where reality fades. Novalis in his 'Fragments' maintains that distance habitually gives rise to poetry since, by distancing, "all becomes romantic". Rodenbach concurs: "It is essential for poets to escape from provincial life, for almost always it is only by having left their country that it then appears to them from a distance as something gentle and beautiful through the mirage of memory." This collection is the bridge to Rodenbach's later work and it introduces the players who will later become familiar to the reader – Bruges, its rain, mist, old quays, crow-stepped gables, convents, processions, canals – but the poet has not yet become totally immersed in the climate of the dead Bruges; he has not quite mastered its atmosphere. As poet Iwan Gilkin said of *The White Youth* at the time of its publication: "It is the song of the bird which has found its nest."

The Reign of Silence of 1891, like the later *The Enclosed Lives*, comprises long cycles of poems: 'The Life of Rooms', 'The Water's Heart', 'Landscapes of Towns', 'Sunday Bells', 'On the Soul's Flow' and 'Of Silence' (one part of 'Of Silence' had been published separately in 1888 by Alphonse Lemerre). In *The Reign of Silence* Rodenbach is in full command of his art. He attempts to create a continuous poem dedicated to the mystical soul of Bruges by maintaining a majestic rhythm and an unbroken flow of numbered, poetically dense meditations on the atmosphere-laden architecture of Bruges, its water, silence, stillness, abandonment and reclusion. Although echoing the withdrawn, reclusive, interiorised world of Maeterlinck's *Serres Chaudes* (1887), the poems in *The Reign of Silence* are not as radical and expressive, nor do they usher in the ground-breaking surrealism of Maeterlinck's images.

In the opening section (poem IV) of 'The Life of Rooms', it is the fading gloxinias and the lifeless piano which serve as objects to initiate the melancholy communication:

"My soul, you suffered and you strained
to see your life, faded too and wilting,
dying with these gentle gloxinias."

Rodenbach muses (in poem VI) that the keys of the piano, silent and abandoned for so long, might be roused to produce former harmonies by the touch of a passing virgin on a spring evening – yet nothing happens; it is but a fanciful dream. Rodenbach revels in both the chimera of romantic awakening and the bitter truth; the isolation of the piano is the isolation of the cheated yet resigned poet. "Night falls; the wind grows colder; no one comes…"

The room appears again in poem VII of 'Of Silence' where entering a hostelry for the night the poet inadvertently disturbs the jealously-guarded silence of a sombre room where

> "Some remnant of an insipid odour floated there still
> of old bouquets mixed with kisses from a distant past,
> but now extinct within invisible glass."

Rodenbach cleverly infuses the mysteriously defunct room with an identity which is immediately sensed by the unwitting visitor on entering:

> "Seized by dread, we went with muffled steps,
> as one enters the room of an invalid…"

Here too the musical instrument is sleeping and the fabrics "of former times" are faded. The silence that has grown here is pervasive and dominating, yet it can be destroyed instantly by the mere whisper of an intruder and, being aware of this, it has become hostile.

Rodenbach's room is not always hostile and forbidding, however; it can also be a space of calmness and relief, disapproving of the one who leaves and welcoming the returning 'absentee', just as Hugues Viane is welcomed as he returns to his rooms after an evening promenade in *Bruges-la-Morte*. In poem XIII of 'The Life of Rooms', the abandoned room finds its voice:

> "the lamps softly opening like eyes,
>
> Like the eyes of the room, filled with reproach
> for the one who searched outside for a futile joy;
> and the curtain folds, that a slow shiver draws closed,
> murmur softly of the wanderer's return."

But as we see in 'The Water's Heart', it is the exterior that generally denotes the threat. In poem X, the town has embalmed itself in its canal waters, water being both a sanctuary for the world-weary and something poisoned by its own darkness now that nobler times are no more. It draws everything around it into its all-encompassing lethargy:

> "and the dead sky lives on in the weary heart,
> the weary water's heart that suddenly has colour
> and imagines fine ladies on its banks forever."

In *The Enclosed Lives*, water is again the subject of poem XII of 'The Invalids at the Windows':

> "The waters of the old canals are sick and enfeebled,
> so mournful, among the dead towns, along the quays
> trimmed by trees and gables in rows, which
> in this impoverished water barely show;
> aged waters lacking fortitude; sickly, deprived
> of all impulsion to steel themselves against the breeze
> that furrows them with too many ripples…"

Here, however, water can be wounded in the same way as silence can, by anything that has movement, energy, a hostile exterior life. In the series 'Mental Aquarium' (poem I) Rodenbach plays with the popularity of the aquarium at the end of the nineteenth century, making water merge with glass and mirrors to create an enclosure which is impervious even to the assault of fish moving languidly about in it, where

> "…even the sun, with its cruel lance blow,
> leaves no further wound in her dark crystal."

The water is protected by "partitions of glass" and because of the mirrors, an enclosed life of great richness is created, an interior life that finds consolation in the aquarium of the mind.

> "she is closed to the world and entirely self-possessed
> and no wind destroys her fragile universe."

Along with his fear of jettisoning the trusty formal rhyme scheme, Rodenbach also pathologically feared modernity, commercial intrusion and the sacrifice of tradition. Where Verhaeren was prepared to embrace the potential positive aspects of progress, Rodenbach saw only existential despair and spiritual sterility. His morbid anxiety about the renovation of Bruges comes to the fore in 'The Landscape of Towns', a poem from *The Reign of Silence*, where he dreads

> "… Murders with pick-axes
> attacking the ancient walls whose great age seemed
> prepared to defend them somehow against these crimes…

> But soon the unanimous hammers will penetrate
> them, ancient walls, yet sacred as the flesh."

One senses through his depiction of this architectural execution the helplessness of the ancient dwellings, where once "youthfulness and love laughed from their windows" as they await their fate.

The Enclosed Lives and *The Mirror of the Native Sky* continue the tone of reclusion and analogy, where images enhance the sense of imprisonment and the allegorical representation of the subconscious. In the poem 'Evening in the Windows', as the golden glow of sunset fades, gathering shadows give rise to an atmosphere of foreboding, and the dwelling and its occupants are suddenly put at risk:

> "something poisonous germinates there,
> threatening this house on the edge of sleep;"

Such images of bewitchment recall Huysmans and his accounts of Satanism in Bruges. In the poem 'The Lines of the Hand' an uncharacteristically wry and playful Rodenbach is evident, yet still the tone is overwhelmingly melancholy as we observe the hand succumb to its fate. At first, the youthful and naïve hand plays unconcernedly in the air "like a bird taunting the ocean's spume" but, having matured, the hand becomes a bejewelled, purse-dipping creature unaware that the myriad lines forming across it signify that "Death is already spinning his spider's web".

A year after the publication of *The Mirror of the Native Sky* and the novel *Le Carillioneur*, Rodenbach was gone. Following his death

Commemorative plaque on George Rodenbach's house at rue Berckmans 93, Saint Gilles, Brussels

there was a collective awareness that a rare spirit, and a man who had been genuinely loved by his peers, had prematurely departed. Camille Mauclair, who wrote the preface to Rodenbach's collected works, said of him: "He was a genuine solitary, a most charming and secretive passer-by. He travelled a great distance down a special path towards a special objective." Thankfully Emile Verhaeren was characteristically more specific:

> "If it were necessary to assign Rodenbach a place in Belgian literature, it would be easy to define. He would stand in the premier rank of those whose sorrow, pain, subtle sentiment and talent nourished by memory, braid a crown of pale violets on the brow of Flanders: Maeterlinck, Van Leberghe, Grégoire le Roy, Max Elskamp. But it seems wiser not to isolate him in a group, not to detach him from the greater French literature of which he was a part. Groupings by country or provinces shrink aesthetic judgements. Art is not based on region, it is of the world."

Will Stone

*L'homme à la rose –
Rodenbach's tomb in Père Lachaise Cemetery, Paris
(Photograph: Will Stone)*

GEORGES RODENBACH
POEMS

DIMANCHES

Morne l'après-midi des dimanches, l'hiver,
Dans l'assoupissement des villes de province,
Où quelque girouette inconsolable grince
Seule, au sommet des toits, comme un oiseau de fer!

Il flotte dans le vent on ne sait quelle angoisse!
De très rares passants s'en vont sur les trottoirs:
Prêtres, femmes du peuple en grands capuchons noirs,
Béguines revenant des saluts de paroisse.

Des visages de femme ennuyés sont collés
Aux carreaux, contemplant le vide et le silence,
Et quelques maigres fleurs, dans une somnolence,
Achèvent de mourir sur les châssis voilés.

Et par l'écartement des rideaux des fenêtres,
Dans les salons des grands hôtels patriciens
On peut voir, sur des fonds de gobelins anciens,
Dans de vieux cadres d'or, les portraits des ancêtres,

En fraise de dentelle, en pourpoint de velours,
Avec leur blason peint dans un coin de la toile,
Qui regardent au loin s'allumer une étoile
Et la ville dormir dans des silences lourds.

tous ces vieux hôtels sont vides et sont ternes;
Le moyen âge mort se réfugie en eux;
C'est ainsi que, le soir, le soleil lumineux
Se réfugie aussi dans les tristes lanternes.

Ô lanternes, gardant le souvenir du feu,
Le souvenir de la lumière disparue,
Si tristes dans le vide et le deuil de la rue
Qu'elles semblent brûler pour le convoi d'un Dieu!

Et voici que soudain les cloches agitées
Ébranlent le Beffroi debout dans son orgueil,
Et leurs sons, lourds d'airain, sur la ville au cercueil
Descendent lentement comme des pelletées!

SUNDAYS

Mournful Sunday afternoons in winter,
in the drowsiness of provincial towns,
where some inconsolable weather cock creaks
alone on a roof-top like a bird of iron!

And drifting on the wind who knows what dread.
Rare passers-by on the pavements:
priests, working women in great black hooded cloaks,
béguines returning from the parish service.

The faces of listless women are pressed
to the pane, gazing on the void and silence,
and a few meagre flowers, settled in somnolence,
perfect their death in the veiled frames.

And in the space between the curtains
in drawing rooms of large patrician mansions
in backgrounds of old gobelin tapestries
in ancient frames of gold, ancestral portraits

in velvet doublet and ruffs of lace,
crests painted in a corner of the canvas,
watch as a star is lit up in the distance
and the town sleeps on in heavy silences.

And all those old mansions are empty, lifeless,
the dead middle ages seek refuge within;
and so it is, at evening, the luminous sun
seeks refuge too in their melancholy lanterns.

O lanterns, guarding the memory of fire,
the memories of light long disappeared,
so dejected in the empty street in mourning
they seem to burn for the cortege of some deity!

And now of a sudden the restless bells
disturb the belfry planted in its pride,
and their sound, heavy with bronze, slowly falls
on the coffin of the town as if in spadefuls.

SEUL

Vivre comme en exil, vivre sans voir personne
Dans l'immense abandon d'une ville qui meurt,
Où jamais l'on n'entend que la vague rumeur
D'un orgue qui sanglote ou du Beffroi qui sonne.

Se sentir éloigné des âmes, des cerveaux
Et de tout ce qui porte au front un diadème;
Et, sans rien éclairer, se consumer soi-même
Tel qu'une lampe vaine au fond de noirs caveaux.

Être comme un vaisseau qui rêvait d'un voyage
Triomphal et joyeux vers le rouge équateur
Et qui se heurte à des banquises de froideur
Et se sent naufrager sans laisser un sillage.

Oh! vivre ainsi! tout seul, tout seul! voir se flétrir
La blanche floraison de son Âme divine,
Dans le dédain de tous et sans qu'aucun devine,
Et seul, seul, toujours seul, se regarder mourir!

ALONE

To live as in exile, to live seeing no-one
in the vast desolation of a town that is dying,
where nothing is heard but the vague murmur
of an organ sobbing, or the belfry tolling.

To feel yourself remote from souls, from minds,
from all that bears a diadem on its brow;
and without shedding light consume yourself
like a futile lamp in the depths of dark burial vaults.

To be like a vessel that dreamed of voyage,
triumphal, cheerful, towards the red equator
which runs into ice floes of coldness
and feels itself wrecked without leaving a wake.

O to live thus! All alone… all alone to witness
the wilting of this divine soul's white flowering,
in contempt of all and without prediction,
alone, alone, always alone, observing one's own extinction.

VIEUX QUAIS

Il est une heure exquise à l'approche des soirs,
Quand le ciel est empli de processions roses
Qui s'en vont effeuillant des âmes et des roses
Et balançant dans l'air des parfums d'encensoirs.

Alors tout s'avivant sous les lueurs décrues
Du couchant dont s'éteint peu à peu la rougeur,
Un charme se révèle aux yeux las du songeur:
Le charme des vieux murs au fond des vieilles rues.

Façades en relief, vitraux coloriés,
Bandes d'Amours captifs dans le deuil des cartouches,
Femmes dont la poussière a défleuri les bouches,
Fleurs de pierre égayant les murs historiés.

Le gothique noirci des pignons se décalque
En escaliers de crêpe au fil dormant de l'eau,
Et la lune se lève au milieu d'un halo
Comme une lampe d'or sur un grand catafalque.

Oh! les vieux quais dormants dans le soir solennel,
Sentant passer soudain sur leurs faces de pierre
Les baisers et l'adieu glacé de la rivière
Qui s'en va tout là-bas sous les ponts en tunnel.

Oh! les canaux bleuis à l'heure où l'on allume
Les lanternes, canaux regardés des amants
Qui devant l'eau qui passe échangent des serments
En entendant gémir des cloches dans la brume.

Tout agonise et tout se tait: on n'entend plus
Qu'un très mélancolique air de flûte qui pleure,
Seul, dans quelque invisible et noirâtre demeure
Où le joueur s'accoude aux châssis vermoulus!

OLD QUAYS

That exquisite hour at evening's approach,
when the heavens fill with processions tinged rose
which advance shedding flowers and souls
casting into the air the fragrance of censers.

Then, more lucid beneath the declining light
of sunset, whose crimson glow gradually fades,
a charm is revealed to the dreamer's jaded eye:
the charm of old walls where ancient streets die.

Façades ornamented, coloured stained glass,
bands of captive cupids in mournful cartouches,
women whose mouths are deflowered by dust,
stone flowers brightening historiated walls.

The black gothic of the gables is traced
on the drowsy current as stairways of crepe
and the moon rises at the halo's core,
a lamp of gold upon a great wooden bier.

O, the old quays slumbering in the solemn dusk
sensing of a sudden on their stone countenance
the kisses and icy farewell of the river
that runs into tunnels beneath the bridges.

O, the bluish shade they acquire at the hour
when lamps are lit, canals gazed on by lovers
at the water's edge, exchanging their vows,
hearing moan through mists, the carillon sound.

All is in the throes of death, all keeps silent:
nothing but a weeping flute's melancholy tune,
alone in some dwelling blackened and unseen,
on whose worm-eaten window-frame the player leans!

Et l'on devine au loin le musicien sombre,
Pauvre, morne, qui joue au bord croulant des toits;
La tristesse du soir a passé dans ses doigts,
Et dans sa flûte à trous il fait chanter de l'ombre.

And one imagines far off, that mournful musician,
crestfallen, impoverished, playing under crumbling eaves;
as into his fingers passes evening's sorrow,
and with his flute he draws song from the shadows.

NOCTURNE

Devant votre maison close dans du silence
Combien je suis allé souvent, par les beaux soirs,
Avec les gestes fous d'un amant qui balance
Ses songes dans le vent comme des encensoirs.

Je n'avais nul espoirs de vous voir apparaître;
Dans vos rideaux à fleurs je vous savais dormant;
Mais je croyais sentir à travers la fenêtre
Quelque chose de vous m'arriver par moment.

Les rangs d'arbres plissaient dans le brouillard des voiles
En processionnant à l'horizon qui fuit;
Et le cortège blanc des divines étoiles
Écoutait le Silence et regardait la Nuit.

A peine entendait-on en de lointaines rues
Les pas lourds d'un veilleur ou l'aboiement d'un chien
Et toutes ces rumeurs incessamment décrues
Évoquaient un eau morte où l'on ne voit plus rien.

Et je restais longtemps, debout, sous vos croisées,
Et mes yeux fatigués s'amusaient à saisir
Le caprice des fleurs de fonte entre-croisées
Aux dessins du balcon où montait mon désir.

Et me sachant tout près de vous dans la nuit calme,
J'imaginais qu'un peu de mon âme en émoi
Devait aller vers vous avec un bruit de palme
Et qu'en ce moment-là vous rêveriez de moi!

NOCTURNE

Before your house enclosed in silence
how often I went, on fine evenings,
with the mad gestures of a lover who sways
his dreams in the wind like censers.

I had no hope of seeing you appear;
I knew you slept behind your flowery curtains;
but across the window I thought I sensed
something of you at certain moments.

Rows of trees folding veils in the mist
all in procession to the horizon in flight;
and the white cortege of sanctified stars
listened to the Silence and observed the Night.

Barely could be heard on the distant roads
a dog's bark or the night watchman's heavy tread
and all these murmurs so quickly worn
evoked a dead water where sight cannot penetrate.

And I stayed a long time, standing, beneath your windows
and my wearied eyes amused themselves picking out
the caprice of iron flowers intertwined
with the balcony outline where my desire climbed.

And knowing I was close to you in a night so calm
I imagined that a little of my aroused soul
must go to you with a palm leaf's sound
and in that very moment you'd dream of me!

DÉPART

La gare du village avait des airs funèbres
Tassant son grand bloc d'ombre au milieu des ténèbres,

Au moment des adieux pleurait le vent du nord,
Et la gare, on eût dit une maison de mort.

Quelques rouges fanaux trouaient le crépuscule
Et tous ces fanaux semblaient remplis de sang qui brûle.

Et tout là-bas, parmi les lointains solennels,
Les rails disparaissaient dans l'ombre des tunnels.

La gare du village avait des airs hostiles
Et les rails allongeaient leur froideur de reptiles.

Tout le long de la voie aux feux phosphorescents
Les fils du télégraphe où parlent les absents,

Chuchotant à distance un rappel aux mémoires,
Alignaient dans la nuit leurs fils de harpes noires.

Et lorsque le convoi l'eut emportée au loin,
Je suis resté longtemps, inerte, dans un coin,

Dans un coin où le vent attristait sa musique
A me sentir au cœur un mal presque physique,

Un mal d'écrasement et d'atroce langueur.
comme si tout le train m'eut passé sur le cœur!

DEPARTURE

The village station had a funereal look
pressing its shadow block into the heart of the dark.

At the moment of farewells the north wind wept,
and the station, you could say resembled a house of death.

A scattering of red signals pierced the dusk
and these lights seemed filled with a burning blood.

And over yonder, in the solemn distances,
into the shadows of tunnels the rails vanished.

The village station had a hostile look
and the rails stretched out with reptilian chill.

All along the path of lights phosphorescent,
telegraph wires where conversed the absent,

whispering from far off to call memories up,
aligned in the night their strings of black harps.

And when the convoy had carried her away
I stayed there a long time, in a corner, motionless,

in a corner where the wind saddened its music
sensing in my heart a near-physical sickness,

a sickness of crushing and dreadful languor.
As if the entire train had passed over my heart!

SOLITUDE

Faut-il fixer toujours des yeux mélancoliques,
Tel qu'un prêtre pensif, sur les choses de l'Art,
Tel qu'un prêtre qui reste agenouillé très tard
Dans son église froide, à veiller des reliques?

Faut-il laisser fleurir les fleurs dans son jardin
Pour conquérir la gloire à travers les risées;
Faut-il laisser passer l'Amour sous ses croisées
Et perdre un bien réel pour un rêve incertain?

Faut-il se murer vif et s'empêcher de vivre?
Et, comme en une forge en feu, faut-il verser
Tous les métaux de l'âme au creuset de son livre?

– Vis seul. C'est un temps dur d'épreuve à traverser,
Mais fais ce sacrifice à ta sublime envie:
Pour vivre après ta mort, sois donc mort dans la vie!

SOLITUDE

Must you fix your gaze always with melancholic eyes,
like a pensive priest, upon the things of Art,
like a priest who remains kneeling very late
to watch over relics, in his cold church?

Must you let flowers blossom in the garden
to win over glory through the mocking laughter;
must you let Love pass beneath your windows
and lose a solid gain for an obscure dream?

Must you wall yourself up alive and cease to live?
And, like a blazing forge, must you pour
all the soul's metals into the crucible of your book?

– Live alone. It's a hard time of ordeals to traverse,
but make this sacrifice to your sublime wish:
to live on after your death, be dead then in life!

LA PASSION

Je dis comme le Christ au jardin des Olives;
«Ô Seigneur, mon âme est triste jusqu'à la mort!»
Ayant beaucoup souffert, je n'ai pas de remords,
Quand je trouve, le soir, que mes mains sont fautives.

Parfums de Madeleine, où vous répandez-vous?
Il est enfin le temps où ma belle jeunesse
Passait – comme Jésus monté sur une ânesse
Et sentant des rameaux caresser ses genoux.

Seigneur! J'entends hurler une foule barbare!
Déjà plus d'un Judas m'a baissé le front
Et je sens dans mon cœur que ma Croix se prépare.

Mais, pour souffrir la haine et supporter l'affront,
Seigneur, donnez-moi donc cet espoir de revivre
Dans la mélancolique éternité du Livre.

THE PASSION

I say like Christ in the Garden of Olives:
"O Lord, my soul is sorrowing unto death!"
having suffered much, I have no regrets,
when I find, at evening, my hands are guilty.

Perfumes of Madeleine, where are you diffusing?
It is finally the time where my beautiful youth
passed by – like Jesus mounted on a donkey
feeling his knees caressed by branches.

Lord! I hear a barbarous herd howl
already more than one Judas has kissed my brow
and I feel in my heart that my cross is prepared.

But, to suffer hate and bear the affront,
Lord, grant me then this hope to live again,
in the melancholic eternity of the Book.

LA VIE DES CHAMBRES

IV

Mon âme, tout ce long et triste après-midi,
A souffert de la mort d'un bouquet, imminente!
Il était, loin de moi, dans la chambre attenante
Où ma peur l'éloigna, déjà presque engourdi,
Bouquet dépérissant de fleurs qu'on croyait sauves
Encor pour tout un jour dans la pitié de l'eau,
Gloxinias de neige avec des galons mauves,
Bouquet qui dans la chambre éteignait son halo
Et se désargentait en ce soir de dimanche!
Mon âme, tu souffris et tu t'ingénias
À voir ta vie, aussi fanée et qui se penche,
Agoniser avec ces doux gloxinias.

Or me cherchant moi-même en cette analogie
J'ai passé cette fin de journée à m'aigrir
Par le spectacle vain et la psychologie
Douloureuse des fleurs pâles qui vont mourir.
Triste vase: hôpital, froide alcôve de verre
Qu'un peu de vent, par la fenêtre ouverte, aère
Mais qui les fait mourir plus vite, en spasmes doux,
Les pauvres fleurs, dans l'eau vaine, qui sont phtisiques,
Répandant, comme en de brusques accès de toux,
Leurs corolles sur les tapis mélancoliques.
Douceur! Mourir ainsi sans heurts, comme on s'endort,
Car les fleurs ne sont pas tristes devant la mort,
Et disparaître avec ce calme crépuscule
Qui d'un jaune rayon à peine s'acidule.

THE LIFE OF ROOMS

IV

My soul, this long and listless afternoon
suffered a bouquet's death, looming.
It was, far from me, in the adjoining room
where my fear banished it, already dulled
that fading bouquet of blooms we thought saved
and good for another day in the water's pity,
gloxinias of snow with braidings of mauve,
bouquet that in the room extinguished its halo
and on that Sunday evening felt its silver fading.
My soul, you suffered and you strained
to see your life, faded too and wilting,
dying with these gentle gloxinias.

Now, seeking myself in this analogy
I spent day's end embittered
by the futile spectacle and painful psychology
of flowers which are doomed to die.
Mournful vase: hospital, cold glass recess
that a murmur of wind through an open window, airs
but which kills them off sooner, in tender spasms,
the helpless flowers, in futile water, consumptive
strewing, as if with sudden fits of coughing,
their corollas upon melancholic carpets.
Gentleness! To die unruffled as one sleeps,
for flowers are not dejected before death,
and to disappear with the restful twilight
which a yellow ray barely acidulates.

VI

Dans l'angle obscur de la chambre, le piano
Songe, attendant des mains pâles de fiancée
De qui les doigts sont sans reproche et sans anneau,
Des mains douces par qui sa douleur soit pansée
Et qui rompent un peu son abandon de veuf,
Car il refrémirait sous des mains élargies
Puisqu'en lui dort encor l'espoir d'un bonheur neuf.
Après tant de silence, après tant d'élégies
Que le deuil de l'ébène enferma si longtemps,
Quelle ivresse si, par un soir doux de printemps,
Quelque vierge attirée à sa mélancolie
Ressuscitait de lui tous les rythmes latents
Gerbe de lis blessés que son jeu lent délie;
Eau pâle du clavier où son geste amusé
– Rafraîchi comme ayant joué dans une eau claire
Ferait surgir un blanc cortège apprivoisé,
Cygnes vêtus de clair de lune en scapulaire,
Cygnes de Lohengrin dans l'ivoire nageant!

Hélas! Le piano reste seul et morose
Et défaille d'ennui par ce soir affligeant
Où dans la chambre meurt une suprême rose.
La nuit tombe; le vent fraîchit; nul n'est venu
Et, résigné parmi cette ombre qui le noie,
Il refoule dans le clavier désormais nu
Les possibilités de musique et de joie!

VI

In the dark corner of the room, the piano
dreams, awaiting a fiancée's pale hands
whose fingers lack reproach or ring,
soft hands through which its wounds are healed
and breaks a little its widower's abandonment,
for it would quiver again beneath spread fingers
whilst within still slumbers the hope of fresh happiness.
After so much silence, so many elegies,
shut in so long by the ebony's mourning,
what ecstasy if, on a soft spring evening
some virgin seduced by its melancholy
aroused from it all latent harmonies:
spray of wounded lilies that her slow playing liberates;
the keyboard's pale waters where her light-hearted playing
– refreshed as though played in clear waters –
would call up a docile white cortege,
swans clothed in the light of a scapular moon,
Lohengrin's swans bathing in an ivory pool.

Alas! The piano stands solitary and morose,
enfeebled with ennui by an evening so afflicted
where, in the bedroom, a supreme rose dies.
Night falls; the wind grows colder; no one comes
and resigned amidst this shadow that drowns it,
it folds back into the keyboard, bare from this moment
of any possibility of joy, of music!

VIII

L'obscurité, dans les chambres, le soir, est une
Irréconciliable apporteuse de craintes;
En deuil, s'habillant d'ombre et de linges de lune,
Elle inquiète; elle a de félines étreintes
Comme une eau des canaux traîtres où l'on se noie
L'obscurité, c'est la tueuse de la joie
Qui dépérit, bouquet de roses transitoires,
Quand elle y verse un peu de ses fioles noires.
L'obscurité s'installe avec le crépuscule;
Elle descend dans l'âme aussi qui s'enténèbre;
Sur le miroir heureux tombe un crêpe funèbre
La clarté, dirait-on, est blessée et recule
Vers la fenêtre où s'offre un linceul de dentelle.
L'ombre est un poison noir, d'une douceur mortelle!
Et voici qu'on frémit d'on ne sait quoi… c'est l'heure
Où le vol libéré des âmes nous effleure;
Ah! Quel trouble! Et les peurs, les peurs dominatrices
Dans les rideaux des lits agitant des fantômes!
Et ces sachets du linge aux sensuels arômes!
Et les lampes, là-bas, rouvrant leurs cicatrices,
Qui vont recommencer à faire saigner l'ombre!
Mais l'ombre se défend contre les lampes frêles,
Épaississant dans les angles sa force sombre
– On écoute les moucherons griller leurs ailes… –
Et l'on soupçonne, à voir mourir les bestioles,
Que c'est l'obscurité qui se venge ainsi d'elles
Pour avoir aimé mieux que ses noires fioles
Le soleil qui revit dans les lampes fidèles!

VIII

Darkness, in the bedrooms at evening, is
the irreconcilable bearer of fears;
in mourning, clothed in shadow and moon linen
it disquiets, has a feline embrace,
as in treacherous canal waters where men drown.
Darkness, the killer of joy, which withers
a bouquet of transitory roses,
when it empties the contents of its black phial.
Darkness, hand in hand with the dusk;
it descends into the soul also turning to shadow,
a funereal crepe falls across the cheerful mirror;
brightness seems blighted and retreats
towards the window offering its shroud of lace.
Shadows are a black poison, with a mortal tenderness
and here one trembles for who knows what... it's the hour
when the liberated flight of souls brush against us;
what anguish! The fears, the overwhelming fears
in the drapes of beds restless with phantoms
and these bags of linen with sensual aromas
and the lamps, reopening their scars,
beginning once more to bleed the shadows.
But the shadow holds out against the fragile lamps,
thickening in the corners its stygian strength
– you hear the tiny flies toast their wings –
and suspect on seeing these insects give in,
that it's the darkness taking revenge on them
for having loved far more than her black phial
the sun rekindled in these faithful lamps.

XIII

Quand on rentre chez soi, délivré de la rue,
Aux fins d'automne où, gris cendré, le soir descend
Avec une langueur qu'il n'a pas encore eue,
La chambre vous accueille alors tel qu'un absent...

Un absent cher, depuis longtemps séparé d'elle,
Dont le visage aimé dormait dans le miroir;
Ô chambre délaissée, ô chambre maternelle
Qui, toute seule, eût des tristesses de parloir.

Mais pour l'enfant prodigue elle n'a que louanges...
L'ombre remue au long des murs silencieux:
C'est le soir nouveau-né qui bouge dans ses langes;
Les lampes doucement s'ouvrent comme des yeux,

Comme les yeux de la chambre, pleins de reproche
Pour celui qui chercha dehors un bonheur vain;
Et les plis des rideaux, qu'un frisson lent rapproche,
Semblent parler entre eux de l'absent qui revint.

La chambre fait accueil; et le miroir lucide
Pour l'absent qui s'y mire, est soudain devenu
Son portrait – grâce à quoi lui-même il élucide
Tant de choses sur son visage mieux connu,
Des choses de son âme obscure qui s'avère
Dans ce visage à la dérive où transparaît
Son identité vraie au fil nu du portrait,
Pastel qui dort dans le miroir comme sous verre!

XIII

When you return home delivered from the street
in late autumn when, ash grey, evening descends
with a languor which it has not yet known,
like one long absent, you are welcomed by the room…

Cherished absentee, too long parted from her
whose beloved face slept in the glass of the mirror;
neglected room, maternal room
who, quite alone, suffers the parlour's dejection.

But she has nothing but praise for her prodigal son…
along her silent walls the shadow runs:
it's a new-born evening stirring in swaddling clothes,
the lamps softly opening like eyes,

Like the eyes of the room, filled with reproach
for the one who searched outside for a futile joy;
and the curtain folds, that a slow shiver draws closed,
murmur softly of the wanderer's return.

The room bids welcome; and the clear mirror
for the absentee who regards himself there, suddenly becomes
his portrait – allowing him clearly to see
so many things in his better-known face,
things of his dark soul visible
on this face adrift where
his true identity shows through,
as the portrait lays him bare.

XV

Songeur, dans de beaux rêves t'absorbant,
La pendule, à l'heure où seul tu médites,
T'afflige avec ses bruits froids, stalactites
Du temps qui s'égoutte et pleure en tombant.

C'est une eau qui filtre en petites chutes
Et soudain se glace aux parois du cœur;
Et cela produit toute une langueur
L'émiettement de l'heure en minutes.

Collier monotone et désenfilé
De qui chaque perle est pareille et noire,
Roulant parmi la chambre sans mémoire;
Piqûres du temps; tic-tac faufilé.

Ah! Qu'elle s'arrête un peu, la pendule!
Toujours l'araignée invisible court
Dans le grand silence, avec un bruit sourd…
Et ce qu'elle mord, et nous inocule!

La peur que demain soit comme aujourd'hui,
Que l'heure jamais ne sonne autre chose:
Un destin réglé dans la chambre close;
Un peu plus de sable au désert d'ennui.

XV

Dreamer, absorbed in wondrous reveries,
the pendulum, at the hour when you ponder alone,
afflicts you with its cold sound, stalactites
of time which drains away, weeping as it drops,

water that seeps in little falls
suddenly freezing the heart's wall;
and it causes a deep languor
as the hour crumbles into minutes.

Necklace unthreaded and monotonous
where each pearl is identical and tenebrous
rolling around a room without memory,
stitches of time; ticking threaded.

Ah! If only it would pause for once, the clock.
Always the unseen spider spinning
in the vast silence, sound muted…
then how she bites and inoculates us!

Fear that tomorrow will be as today
that the hour will never chime otherwise:
one's fate ruled in the enclosed room,
just a little more sand on the desert of boredom.

LE COEUR DE L'EAU

X

Les pièces d'eau, songeant dans les parcs taciturnes,
Dans les grands parcs muets semés de boulingrins,
S'aigrissent; et n'ont plus pour tromper leurs chagrins
Qu'un décalque de ciel avant les deuils nocturnes;
Une fête galante en nuages mirés,
En nuages vêtus de satin soufre et rose
Qui s'avancent noués de rubans et parés
Pour quelque menuet ou quelque apothéose:
Nuages du couchant en souples falbalas;
Atours bouffants, paniers sur des hanches aiguës,
Tout se mire parmi les vasques exiguës;
Et le siècle défunt revit dans le coeur las,
Dans le coeur las de l'eau qui soudain se colore
Et croit revoir de belles dames sur ses bords

Le coeur de l'eau des pièces d'eau se remémore,
Lui qui songeait: «ah ! Qu'il est loin le temps d'alors,
Le joli temps des fins corsages à ramages!»
Or ce temps recommence et l'eau revoit encor
Mais pour un court instant, l'ancien et cher décor,
Souvenir qui repasse au hasard des nuages...
Car c'est tout simplement cela, le souvenir:
Un mirage éphémère – une pitié des choses
Qui dans notre âme vide ont l'air de revenir;
Tel, dans les pièces d'eau, le ciel en robes roses!

THE WATER'S HEART

    X

Ponds of water, dreaming in darkened parks,
in the great silent parks sown with lawns,
embittered; with nothing to delude their grief
but a tracing-paper sky before nocturnal mourning;
in mirrored clouds a courtly feast,
clouds dressed in sulphur and pink
which advance tied in trimmings and ribbons
for some apotheosis or minuet:
in soft frills clouds of sunset
full finery, baskets on slender hips
in the exiguous confines of the ponds, where all is reflected,
and the dead sky lives on in the weary heart,
the weary water's heart that suddenly has colour
and imagines fine ladies on its banks forever.

The heart of the pools' water recollects,
he who dreamed: 'Ah, how distant now that time,
the charming time of leaf-patterned bodices.'
Now that time starts afresh and the water still sees it
just for a moment, the cherished setting, timeworn
memory that passes by aimlessly like clouds...
For it's simply that, memory:
Ephemeral mirage – a pity of things
which to our vacant soul seem to return;
as in the ponds of water, the sky in pink gowns.

XI

L'eau, pour qui souffre, est une sœur de charité
Que n'a pu satisfaire aucune joie humaine
Et qui se cache, douce et le sourire amène,
Sous une guimpe et sous un froc d'obscurité;
Son amour du repos, son dégoût de la vie
Sont si contagieux que plus d'un l'a suivie
Dans la chapelle d'ombre, au fond pieux des eaux,
Où, tranquille, elle chante au pied des longs roseaux
Dont l'orgue aux verts tuyaux l'accompagne en sourdine.

Elle chante! Elle dit: «Les doux abris que j'ai
Pour ceux de qui le cœur est trop découragé...»
Ah! La molle attirance et quelle voix divine!
Car, pour leur fièvre, c'est la fraîcheur d'un bon lit!
Et beaucoup, aimantés par cet appel propice,
Perclus, entrent dans l'eau comme on entre à l'hospice,
Puis meurent. L'eau les lave et les ensevelit
Dans ses courants aussi frais que de fines toiles;
Et c'est enfin vraiment pour eux la Bonne mort.
Ce pendant que, le soir, autour du corps qui dort,
L'eau noire allume un grand catafalque d'étoiles.

XII

Le long des quais, sous la plaintive mélopée
Des cloches, l'Eau déserte est tout inoccupée
Et s'en va sous les ponts, silencieusement,
Pleurant sa peine et son immobile tourment,
Se plaindre de la vie éparse qui l'afflige!
Et la lune a beau choir comme une fleur sans tige
Dans le courant, elle a l'air d'être morte, et rien
Ne fait plus frissonner au souffle aérien
Ce pâle tournesol de lumière figée.

XI

The water, for those who suffer, is a sister of charity
unwilling to be satisfied by any human happiness,
who hides herself away, softly and her smile so affable
beneath a wimple and a habit of darkness;
her disgust with life, her adoration of inertia
so contagious that more than one has followed her
into the chapel of shadows, into the pious depth of waters
where, restful, she sings at the long reeds' root,
whose organ of green pipes provides muted accompaniment.

She sings. She says: "Gentle sanctuary I offer
for those whose hearts are too dispirited…"
Oh, the soft attraction and what hallowed voice!
In their fevers it's the freshness of a fine bed.
And many, drawn by this auspicious call,
paralysed, enter the waters as one enters a hospice door
then die. The water washes them, shrouds them
in her currents fresh as delicate cloth;
and for them, in the end it's a *Good* Death.
Whilst at evening, about the sleeping corpse,
black waters kindle a vast catafalque of stars.

XII

Along the quays, beneath the plaintive threnody
of bells, the abandoned water is idle
and flows beneath bridges in silence,
weeping over its grief and inert torments,
lamenting the scattered life that afflicts it
and the moon falls heavy as a bloom without a stem
on the current, she seems dead
and no ephemeral breath will make quiver
this pale sunflower of frozen radiance.

Eau dédaigneuse! Soeur de mon âme affligée,
Qui se refuse aux vains décalques d'alentour,
Elle qui peut pourtant mirer toute une tour
O taciturne coeur! Coeur fermé de l'eau noire.
Toute à se souvenir en sa vaste mémoire
D'un ancien temps vécu qui maintenant est mort:
Cadavre qu'elle lave avec son eau qui tord
Des tristesses de linge en pitié quotidienne
O l'eau, soeur de mon âme, empire des noyés,
Se répétant le soir l'une à l'autre: «Voyez
S'il est une douleur comparable à la mienne!»

Contemptuous water! My afflicted soul's sister
refusing to lose herself to the tracings around her,
she who could yet reflect a whole tower…
Oh silent heart! Closed-in heart of black water,
all recounted in her vast memory
of an ancient time lived that now is dead:
body that she washes with her water that wrings
sorrows from linen into daily pity…
Oh water, sister of my soul, empire of the drowned,
repeating at evening one to the other:
Let's see if it compares to mine, this torture!

PAYSAGES DE VILLE

IV

Dans quelque ville morte, au bord de l'eau, vivote
La tristesse de la vieillesse des maisons
À genoux dans l'eau froide et comme en oraisons;
Car les vieilles maisons ont l'allure dévote,
Et, pour endurer mieux les chagrins qu'elles ont,
Égrènent les pieux carillons qui leur sont
Les grains de fer intermittents d'un grand rosaire.
Vieilles maisons, en deuil pour quelque anniversaire,
Et qui, tristes, avec leurs souvenirs divers,
N'accueillent plus qu'un peu de pauvres et de prêtres.
Ce pendant qu'autrefois, avant les durs hivers,
La jeunesse et l'amour riaient dans leurs fenêtres
Claires comme des yeux qui n'ont pas vu mourir!
Mais, depuis lors, ces yeux des pensives demeures
Dans leurs vitres d'eau frêle ont senti dépérir
Tant de visages frais, tant de guirlandes d'heures
Qu'ils en ont maintenant la froideur de la mort.

(Or mes yeux sont aussi les vitres condamnées
D'une maison en deuil du départ des années)
Et c'est pourquoi, du fond de ces lointains du nord,
Je me sens regardé par ces yeux sans envie
Qui ne se tournent plus du côté de la vie
Mais sont orientés du côté du tombeau...

Yeux des vieilles maisons dont mes yeux sont les frères,
Lassés depuis longtemps des bonheurs temporaires,
Yeux plus touchants près de mourir! Regard plus beau
De ces maisons qu'on va détruire en des jours proches!
Ô profanation! Meurtres avec les pioches
Abattant les vieux murs de qui l'âge avait l'air
De devoir les défendre un peu contre ces crimes...
Mais bientôt entreront les marteaux unanimes
Dans les vieux murs, pourtant sacrés comme une chair.

LANDSCAPES OF TOWNS

IV

In some dead town, at the water's edge, there resides
the grief of ageing houses,
kneeling in cold waters as if in prayer;
for the ancient houses have the look of the devout
and to better endure the sorrows they bear,
count out the pious carillons, which to them are
the intermittent iron beads of a giant rosary.
Ancient houses, in mourning for some anniversary,
and whom, dejected, with their assortment of memories,
welcome only a scattering of paupers and priests.
Yet, in another time, before the hard winters,
youthfulness and love laughed from their windows,
clear as eyes that have never looked upon death's shadow!
But, since then, the eyes of these pensive dwellings
in their panes of frail water have felt wither
so many fresh faces, so many garlands of hours,
that now they have taken on the coldness of death.

(Now my eyes too are condemned panes
of a house in mourning for departed years)
and that's why, from the depths of the distance,
I feel watched by these desireless eyes
that turn no more towards life,
but face the way of the sepulchre...

My eyes are brothers to those of the ancient houses,
weary for so long of temporary joyfulness,
eyes more moving when near to death. Lovelier gaze
of these houses so soon to be destroyed.
Sacrilege! Murders with pick-axes
attacking the ancient walls whose great age seemed
prepared to defend them somehow against these crimes...
But soon the unanimous hammers will penetrate
them, ancient walls, yet sacred as the flesh.

VI

Sur l'horizon confus des villes, les fumées
Au-dessus des murs gris et des clochers épars
Ondulent, propageant en de muets départs
Les tristesses du soir en elles résumées.
On dirait des aveux aux lèvres des maisons:
Chuchotement de brume, inscription en fuite,
Confidence du feu des âtres qui s'ébruite
Dans le ciel et raconte en molles oraisons
L'histoire des foyers où la cendre est éteinte.

Vague mélancolie au loin se propageant...
Car, parmi la langueur d'une cloche qui tinte,
On dirait des ruisseaux d'eau pâle voyageant
Des ruisseaux de silence aux rives non précises
Dont le peu d'eau glisse au hasard, d'un cours mal sûr,
En méandres ridés, en courbes indécises
Et, comme dans la mer, va se perdre en l'azur!

C'est parce qu'on les sait ainsi tout éphémères
Qu'on les suit dans le ciel avec des yeux meilleurs;
Elles que rien n'attache, elles qui vont ailleurs
Et dont les convois blancs emportent nos chimères
Comme dans de la ouate et dans des linges fins.
Évanouissement et dispersion lente
De la fumée au fond du ciel doux, par les fins
D'après-midi, lorsque le vent la violente,
Elle déjà si faible et qui meurt sans effort
– Neige qui fond ; encens perdu dans une église;
Poussière du chemin qui se volatilise, –
Comme une âme glissant du sommeil dans la mort!

VI

On the blurred horizon of towns, smoke
over grey walls and scattered bells
swaying, spreading in mute departures
evening's sorrow embodied in them.
On the lips of houses it seems like a confession:
Fleeting inscriptions, murmurs of mists,
confidence in secrets of the hearth, that spreads
into the skies and tells in soft oration
the story of homes where ash lies cold.

Veiled melancholy in the distance extends...
for within the languor of a bell that sounds
they seem streams of pale water journeying down
streams of silence between veiled banks
where a little water glides by aimlessly, course unsure,
in meandering ripples, in vacillating curves
and as to the sea, flows on to lose itself in skies of blue.

It's because you know they are fleeting
that you follow them in the sky with the keenest eyes;
nothing can hold them, they who pass elsewhere
and whose white convoys bear our chimeras
as if in cotton wool, or delicate linen.
Fading away and slow dispersion
of smoke to the depths of soft heaven, to the close
of afternoon, when the wind assaults it,
already so frail, that without effort dies away
– snow that melts; incense lost in a church;
dust of the road that vanished into thin air, –
like a soul slipping from sleep into death!

XI

En des quartiers déserts de couvents et d'hospices,
Des quartiers d'exemplaire et stricte piété,
Je sais des murs en deuil vieillis sous les auspices
D'un calvaire où s'étale un christ ensanglanté :
Plantée en ses cheveux, la couronne d'épines
Forme un buisson de clous, – le corps est en ruines,
Livide, comme si la lance, l'éraflant,
Avait jauni de fiel sa chair inoculée ;
Les yeux sont de l'eau morte ; et la plaie à son flanc
Est pareille au cœur noir d'une rose brûlée…
– Œuvre barbare et sombre où le supplicié
Pend sur le bois noueux d'un gibet mal scié.

Or cette impression de calvaire subsiste
Lorsque le soir en longs crêpes tissés descend ;
Puisqu'on croit voir, au loin, dans le ciel qui s'attriste
Surgir la nuit où perle une sueur de sang,
Si bien que l'on dirait la nuit crucifiée !
Car les étoiles sont des clous de cruauté
Qui, s'enfonçant dans sa chair nue et défiée,
Lui font des trous et des blessures de clarté !
Ah ! Cette passion qui toujours recommence !
Ce ciel que l'ombre ceint d'épines chaque soir !
Et soudain, comme au coup d'une invisible lance,
La lune est une plaie ouverte à son flanc noir.

XI

In the deserted districts of convents and hospices,
districts of exemplary and rigid piety,
I know walls in mourning aged under the auspices
of a Calvary where a blood-soaked Christ is laid:
In his hair the crown of thorns is planted
forming a bush of nails, – the body a wreck,
livid, as if the spear in grazing it
had yellowed with gall his flesh;
the eyes are of dead water; and the wound in his flank
is like the dark heart of a rose charred black...
– barbarous and sombre work where the martyr
hangs on the gnarled wood of a rough-hewn gibbet.

Now this Calvary impression persists
when evening in long woven crepe descends;
while you seem to see, far off, in the sorrowing heavens
night looming, on which beads of a bloody sweat form,
so you'd think night itself were crucified.
For the stars are the nails of cruelty
which, sinking into bare undaunted flesh,
leave their holes and wounds of brightness.
Ah, that passion which always begins anew.
This sky the shadows gird with thorns at nightfall,
until suddenly, like the blow of a spear unseen,
on her dark flank the moon is a gaping wound.

XIV

C'est tout là-bas, parmi le nord où tout est mort:
Des beffrois survivant dans l'air frileux du nord;

Les beffrois invaincus, les beffrois militaires,
Montés comme des cris vers les ciels planétaires;

Eux dont les carillons sont une pluie en fer,
Eux dont l'ombre à leur pied met le froid de la mer!

Or, moi, j'ai trop vécu dans le nord; rien n'obvie
À cette ombre à présent des beffrois sur ma vie.

Partout cette influence et partout l'ombre aussi
Des autres tours qui m'ont fait le cœur si transi;

Et toujours tel cadran, que mon absence pleure,
Répandant dans mes yeux l'avancement de l'heure,

Tel cadran d'autrefois qui m'hallucine encor,
Couronne d'où, sur moi, s'effeuille l'heure en or!

XIV

Up there in the North, where everything is dead,
belfries still surviving in the cold northern air;

belfries unvanquished, military belfries,
ascending like cries to the planetary heavens;

those whose carillons are a drizzle of iron,
whose shadow spreads from their foot the chill of the ocean.

As for me, I've known the North too long; nothing now
dispels this shadow of the belfries over my existence.

Everywhere shadows and everywhere this influence
of the other towers that so numbed my heart;

and always such a clock face, that my absence mourns for,
bringing to my eyes the hours' advancement,

some clock face of the past that sets me dreaming,
crown from where, over me, the hour in gold is shed.

CLOCHES DE DIMANCHE

II

Le dimanche est toujours tel que dans notre enfance:
Un jour vide, un jour triste, un jour pâle, un jour nu;
Un jour long comme un jour de jeûne et d'abstinence
Où l'on s'ennuie ; où l'on se semble revenu
D'un beau voyage en un pays de gaîté verte,
Encore dérouté dans sa maison rouverte
Et se cherchant de chambre en chambre tout le jour…
Or le dimanche est ce premier jour de retour!

Un jour où le silence, en neige immense, tombe;
Un jour comme anémique, un jour comme orphelin
Ayant l'air d'une plaine avec un seul moulin
Géométriquement en croix comme une tombe.
Il se remontre à moi tel qu'il s'étiolait
Naguère, ô jour pensif qui pour mes yeux d'enfance
Apparaissait sous la forme d'une nuance:
Je le voyais d'un pâle et triste violet,
Le violet du demi-deuil et des évêques,
Le violet des chasubles du temps pascal.
Dimanches d'autrefois! Ennui dominical
Où les cloches, tintant comme pour des obsèques,
Propageaient dans notre âme une peur de mourir.

Or toujours le dimanche est comme aux jours d'enfance:
Un étang sans limite, où l'on voit dépérir
Des nuages parmi des moires de silence.
Dimanche: une tristesse, un émoi sans raison…
Impression d'un blanc bouquet mélancolique
Qui meurt; impression tristement angélique
D'une petite sœur malade en la maison…

SUNDAY BELLS

II

Sundays are always like those of childhood:
An empty day, a sad day, a pale day, a bare day;
a long day like a day of fasting and abstinence –
of boredom; where you feel you have returned
from a wonderful journey in a land of green gaiety,
but still diverted in your reopened house
and seeking yourself room by room from dawn…
Sunday is this first day of return!

A day where silence, in boundless snow, falls;
an anaemic day, a day like an orphan
with the air of a plain and a solitary windmill
its sails a geometric cross as over a gravestone.
It shows itself to me the way it faded away
in times past, that pensive day, which to my child's eyes
appeared as if in the form of a nuance:
I saw it as a pale and sorrowful violet,
the violet of half-mourning and bishops,
the violet of Eastertide chasubles.
Sundays of times past, tedium of the dominical
where the bells chimed as if for funerals,
spreading over our souls a dread of death.

Now Sunday is always like the days of childhood:
a measureless pond, where one sees fade
clouds amidst shimmering ripples of silence;
Sunday: a grief, an agitation without reason…
impression of a melancholic white bouquet
that dies; impression sorrowfully angelic
of a little sister in the house fallen sick…

V

Tel dimanche pour moi s'embaume de la voix
Des soprani, s'ouvrant comme une cassolette
Dans quelque église. Ô voix doucement aigrelette;
Chant comme tuyauté, comme raide d'empois,
Évoquant des rochets plissés de séminaires.
Tout à coup l'orgue exulte et roule ses tonnerres
Puis se tait; et le chant des soprani reprend,
Chant frêle, chant mouillé parmi la vaste église,
Montant dans le silence et le réfrigérant
De son mince jet d'eau qui se volatilise...

L'orgue encor recommence à hisser ses velours
Qui s'éployent à grands plis sonores dans l'abside;
Puis un autre motet frêlement se décide
Et s'entr'aperçoit vague entre les piliers lourds.
Oh! Si vague, on dirait un cierge qui s'allume;
Ce n'est pas un oiseau; c'est à peine une plume
Qui vacille dans le vent doux des encensoirs...

Et l'orgue de nouveau hisse ses velours noirs.

Or en les entendant, ces voix insexuelles,
On songe aux vieux tableaux, on songe aux chérubins
Qu'en des assomptions les primitifs ont peints,
Des chérubins n'ayant qu'une tête et des ailes,
Enfants-fleurs d'un jardin quasi-religieux,
Envolement de lis devenant des colombes...

Ah! Ces chants d'innocence, et si contagieux!
Linges frais par-dessus la fièvre de nos lombes...

V

Sunday for me is embalmed with the voice
of a soprano, opening like a cassolette
in some ancient church. Oh voice softly shrill;
song as if from pipes, as though starch-stiffened
evoking the pleated albs of seminaries.
Suddenly the organ exults and rolls its thunder,
then is silent and the soprano takes over,
frail song, song dampened in the vast church,
ascending in the silence and cooling it
with a thin water jet that vanishes...

Again the organ sounds, hauling up its velvet
that spreads through the apse in great echoing folds;
then another motet frailly resolves
and between heavy pillars half appears
so vague, you might think it a candle lighting;
this is no bird; it's scarcely a feather
that oscillates in the gentle breeze of censers...

Once more the organ hauls up its dark velvet.

Now you hear them, these androgynous voices,
you dream of old paintings, of cherubim
that the primitives placed in assumptions,
cherubim having only head and wings,
infant-blooms in a near religious garden
flight of lilies becoming doves...

Ah, so contagious! These songs of innocence,
cool linen lowered upon the fever of our loins...

XII

Le dimanche est un ciel vide et silencieux
Où j'écoute frémir les coiffes des béguines
Dont la marche aboutit à mon cœur anxieux.
Halo de bruit autour des faces ivoirines,
Halo de bruit malgré l'absence m'arrivant...
Ah! Cela vient vers moi de si loin dans le vent
Ces frissons de cornette en forme de colombe
Quelque chose de blanc qui sur les fronts surplombe:
Ailes faites de neige et de linge qui dort,
Ailes faites aussi d'un peu de clair de lune
Qui paraissent, ayant replié leur essor,
Être le saint-esprit descendu sur chacune!

Car les béguines sont les sœurs du saint-esprit;
Et leurs calmes couvents, dans les enclos gothiques,
Ne sont-ce pas plutôt des colombiers mystiques?
Essaims d'âmes (encore un peu, Dieu les proscrit)
Qui se reposent là, dans des haltes bénignes,
En picorant les grains bénits des chapelets;
Mais s'en iront bientôt par les soirs violets
Sur leurs ailes de linge aux blancheurs rectilignes.

XII

Sunday is a sky of emptiness and silence
where I listen to the quivering caps of the béguines
whose walk ends at my anxious heart.
Halo of sound around faces of ivory,
halo of sound despite absence approaching me…
Ah, it comes to me on the wind from far off
these quiverings of cornets in the form of a dove:
Something of white that overhangs brows,
wings made of snow and linen that sleeps,
wings even formed from a little moonlight
that appear, having refolded their flight,
to be the Holy Spirit descending on each.

For the béguines are the sisters of Saint-Esprit;
and their calm convents, in gothic enclosures,
are they not rather mystical dovecotes?
Swarms of souls (any more and God would exile them)
who repose there, in benign recess,
pecking at consecrated rosary beads;
but on violet evenings will take their leave
on linen wings of rectilinear whiteness.

AU FIL DE L'ÂME

I

Ne plus être qu'une âme au cristal aplani
Où le ciel propagea ses calmes influences;
Et, transposant en soi des sons et des nuances,
Mêler à leurs reflets une part d'infini.
Douceur! C'est tout à coup une plainte de flûte
Qui dans cette eau de notre âme se répercute;
Là meurt une fumée ayant des bleus d'encens...
Ici chemine un bruit de cloche qui pénètre
Avec un glissement de béguine ou de prêtre,
Et mon âme s'emplit des roses que je sens...
Au fil de l'âme flotte un chant d'épithalame;
Puis je reflète un pont debout sur des bruits d'eaux
Et des lampes parmi les neiges des rideaux...
Que de reflets divers mirés au fil de l'âme!

Mais n'est-ce pas trop peu? N'est-ce pas anormal
Qu'aucun homme ne soit arrivé de la ville
Pour ajouter sa part de mirage amical
Aux choses en reflets dans notre âme tranquille?
Nulle présence humaine et nul visage au fil
De cette âme qui n'a reflété que des cloches.
Ah! Sentir tout à coup la tiédeur d'un profil,
Des yeux posés sur soi, des lèvres vraiment proches.
Fraternelle pitié d'un passant dans le soir
Par qui l'on n'est plus seul, par qui vit le miroir!

ON THE SOUL'S FLOW

I

To be no more than a soul of smooth crystal
where the sky unfurled her peaceful influences;
and, transposing into oneself sounds and nuances,
to mix in their reflections a measure of the infinite.
Softness! Suddenly a flute's lament
in this water of our soul is sent back;
there, an incense-blue smoke dies away...
Here the sound of a bell penetrates
with the gliding of a béguine or priest,
and my soul fills with the scent of roses...
On the soul's flow floats a song of epithalamium;
then I reflect a bridge above the noise of waters
and lamps amidst the snow of curtains...
On the soul's flow what myriad reflections!

But are these too few? Is it not abnormal
that no man has come from the town
to add his share of the friendly mirage
to things reflected in our peaceful souls?
No human presence and no face on the flow
of this soul which reflected nothing but bells.
Ah, to feel suddenly the scant warmth of a profile,
eyes resting on you, lips truly close...
Brotherly pity of a passer-by at dusk
through whom one is less alone, through whom the mirror lives!

IX

Aux vitres de notre âme apparaissent le soir
Des visages anciens demeurés dans le verre;
Leur souvenir, malgré le temps, y persévère,
Visages du passé qu'on souffre de revoir:
Fronts sans cesse pâlis; lèvres déveloutées;
Yeux couverts chaque jour d'ombres surajoutées
Et qui dans la mémoire achèvent de mourir...
Visage d'une mère ou visage de femme
Qui jadis ont vécu le plus près de notre âme.
Encor si l'on pouvait un peu les refleurir
Ces faces, dans le verre, à peine nuancées
Et voir distinctement leurs traits dans nos pensées!
Faces mortes toujours près de s'évanouir
Et sans cesse émergeant, – sitôt qu'on les oublie, –
Au fil de l'âme, en des détresses d'Ophélie
Dont les cheveux de lin ont un air de rouir...
Ah! Comment essayer d'avoir un peu de joie
Quand les vitres de l'âme aimante sont de l'eau
Où reparaît sans cesse et sans cesse se noie
Un doux visage intermittent dans un halo!

IX

In the panes of our soul appear at dusk
ancient faces that dwell in the glass;
their memory, in spite of time, endures there,
faces of the past that you suffer to see again:
Brows grown forever pale; their lips' velvet gone;
eyes covered each day with added shadows
and which in memory draw towards death...
Face of a mother or the face of a woman
who once lived closest to our soul.
Yet if we could just add bloom a little
to these faces, barely made out, in the glass,
and discern clearly their features in our thoughts.
Dead faces always close to fading
and endlessly emerging – as soon as you forget them –
on the soul's flow, in the distresses of Ophelia
whose flaxen locks appear to rust...
Ah, how to secure a scrap of pleasure
when the panes of the loving soul are of water,
where endlessly reappears and endlessly drowns
intermittent, a gentle face in a halo.

DU SILENCE

I

Silence: c'est la voix qui se traîne, un peu lasse,
De la dame de mon silence, à très doux pas
Effeuillant les lis blancs de son teint dans la glace;
Convalescente à peine, et qui voit tout là-bas
Les arbres, les passants, des ponts, une rivière
Où cheminent de grands nuages de lumière,
Mais qui, trop faible encore, est prise tout à coup
D'un ennui de la vie et comme d'un dégoût
Et, – plus subtile, étant malade, – mi-brisée,
Dit: «Le bruit me fait mal; qu'on ferme la croisée...»

VII

La chambre avait un air mortuaire et fermé
Dans cette hôtellerie, en une ville morte,
Où nous avons vécu, ce divin soir de mai!
Silencieusement se referma la porte,
Comme en peine de voir entrer notre bonheur.
Et nous allions à pas étouffés, pris de peur,
Comme on entre dans la chambre d'une malade...
Il flottait quelque chose encor d'une odeur fade
D'anciens bouquets mêlés jadis à des baisers
Et maintenant défunts en d'invisibles verres.
Et les sombres rideaux aux plis éternisés
Et les meubles d'un luxe âgé, froids et sévères,
Gardaient sur eux de la poussière en flocons noirs
Qui parmi l'autrefois des étoffes fanées
Mélancoliquement, depuis tant de longs soirs,
Avaient neigé du lent sablier des années!

Chambre étrange: on eût dit qu'elle avait un secret
D'une chose très stricte et dont elle était lasse
D'avoir vu le mystère en fuite dans la glace!...

OF SILENCE

I

Silence: the voice that drags itself, a little weary
from the lady of my silence, with very soft tread;
shedding in the mirror the white lilies of her complexion
the barely convalescent who sees all out there
the trees, passers-by, bridges, a river
where great clouds of light travel,
but who, still too frail, is suddenly seized
by the weariness of life and with a disgust
and – more subtle, being ill – half broken,
says: 'Noise wounds me; close the window…'

VII

The atmosphere in the room was inscrutable, funereal
in that hostelry in a dead town,
where we lived that divine May evening.
Silently the door closed behind us,
as if barely able to watch our joy pass.
Seized by dread we went with muffled steps,
as one enters the room of an invalid…
Some remnant of an insipid odour floated there still
of old bouquets mixed with kisses from a distant past,
but now extinct within invisible glass.
The dark curtains with lingering folds
and furniture of spent luxury, severe and cold,
retained the dust in black flakes
that amidst the faded fabrics of former times
dejectedly, over so many long evenings,
had snowed from the slow hourglass of the years.

Curious room: you would think it guarded a secret
of something mournful and of which it wearied
from having seen the mystery fleeing in the glass…

Car notre amour faisait du mal à son regret.
Et même lorsque avec des mains presque dévotes
Tu vins frôler le vieux clavecin endormi,
Ce fut un chant si pâle et si dolent parmi
La solitude offerte au réveil des gavottes
Que tu tremblas comme au contact d'un clavier mort.
Et muets, nous sentions, dans cette chambre étrange
Avec qui notre joie était en désaccord,
L'hostilité d'un grand silence qu'on dérange!

XIV

Chagrin d'être un sans gloire qui chemine
Dans le grand parc d'octobre délabré,
Chagrin encor de s'être remembré
Le printemps vert que le vent dissémine,

Le vent qui pleure, au loin, comme un tambour
Battant l'appel des anciennes années…
Et l'on se sent, dans l'exil du faubourg,
Les yeux aussi pleins de choses fanées.

Et, bien qu'en la jeunesse encore-on croit
Que son printemps a presque un air d'automne,
Avec l'ennui d'un jet d'eau monotone
Dont la chanson, comme un amour, décroît.

Et, triste à voir le vent froid qui balance
Des fils de la vierge fins et frileux,
On s'imagine en ce parc de silence
Que ces fils blancs entrent dans les cheveux.

For our love did harm to its regret.
And even when, with hands near devoted
you brushed against the harpsichord that slept,
there was a song so pale and mournful amidst
the solitude offered to the rousing of gavottes
that, as if touching a lifeless keyboard, you trembled.
And mute we felt in that strange room
with which our joy was in disaccord,
the hostility of the great silence we disturbed.

    XIV

Grief of one lacking glory who moves
through the vast decayed park in October,
a grief as well to remember
the green springtime the wind scatters.

The wind that weeps, in the distance, like a drum
beating the call of years long gone…
And one senses in the exile of a suburb,
eyes also filled with things long faded.

And though still in youth – one thinks
his spring almost has the feel of autumn,
with a monotonous water jet's boredom
whose song, like a love, declines.

And so sad to see the chill wind that sways
threads so sensitive and delicate,
you imagine in this park of silence
they get into the hair, these white gossamers.

XXI

Très défuntes sont les maisons patriciennes
Et très dorénavant closes dans du silence
Parmi des quartiers froids, en des villes anciennes,
Où les pignons, pris d'une inerte somnolence,
Ne voient plus rien de grand, dans le soir diaphane,
Qui descende sur eux du soleil qui se fane;
Et, pour fleurir le deuil de ces vieilles demeures
Qui sont les tombeaux noirs des choses disparues,
Seul le carillon lent sème tous les quarts d'heures
Ses lourdes fleurs de fer dans le vide des rues!

XXII

Les canaux somnolents entre les quais de pierre
Songent, entre les quais rugueux, comme en exil,
Sans paysage clair qui se renverse au fil
De l'eau qui rêve, – ainsi s'isole une âme fière, –
L'âme de l'eau captive entre les quais dormants
Où le ciel se transpose en pensive nuance
Dont la douceur à du silence se fiance.
Quelques nuages seuls cheminent par moments
Dans les canaux muets aux eaux inanimées
Qui semblent des miroirs réflétant des fumées.
Puis le ciel s'unifie, incolore et profond,
Et les pâles canaux entre leurs quais de pierre
Sont sans mirage, – ainsi dédaigne une âme fière, –
Et tout passage d'aile en leur cristal se fond;
Plus rien n'entre parmi leurs eaux coagulées
Dont la blancheur ressemble à des vitres gelées
Derrière qui l'on voit, dans le triste du soir,
L'âme de l'eau, captive au fond, qui persévère
À ne rien regretter du monde en son lit noir
Et qui semble dormir dans des chambres de verre!

XXI

Utterly extinct are the patrician mansions
and from now on rigidly enclosed in silence
within cold districts, in old towns,
where the gables, seized by inert drowsiness,
see no more of greatness in diaphanous evening
that descends to them from a fading sun;
and, to bring into blossom these old dwellings' mourning,
these sombre tombs of all that has passed,
the carillon alone slowly sows each quarter hour
in the desert of the street her heavy iron flowers.

XXII

Between quays of stone dream the drowsy canals,
between rough worn quays, as if in exile,
no bright landscape inversed on the flow
of the dreaming water, – thus a proud soul is isolated –
between sleeping quays soul of the water held captive
where the sky is transposed in reflective nuance
whose softness is betrothed to silence.
A few lone clouds pass at intervals
in the lifeless waters of the silent canals,
which seem like mirrors reflecting smoke.
Then the sky comes together, colourless and deep
and the pale canals between their stone quays
are bereft of mirage – thus a proud soul disparages –
and all motion of wings in their crystal merges;
nothing more enters their curdled waters
whose whiteness resembles frosted panes
behind which you see, in evening's sadness,
the water's soul, depths held captive, who strives
to regret nothing of the world on her bed so dark
and who seems to sleep on in rooms of glass.

XXIII

Mon rêve s'en retourne en souvenirs tranquilles
Vers votre humilité, vieilles petites villes,
Villes de mon passé, villes élégiaques,
Si dolentes les soirs de noël et de pâques,
Villes aux noms si doux: Audenarde, Malines,
Pieuses, qui priez comme des ursulines
En rythmant des avé sur les carillons tristes!
Oh! Villes de couvents, villes de catéchistes,
Avec la sainte odeur des encens et des cires,
Villes s'assoupissant, si doucement martyres
De n'avoir pas été suffisamment aimées,
Qui, dégageant le gris mourant de leurs fumées
Comme une plainte d'âme exténuée et vierge,
Agonisent dans le brouillard qui les submerge.

Ensommeillement doux de mes villes natales
Que, le soir, je retrouve en des marches mentales;
Mais, le long des vieux quais, ô mon rêve, où tu erres,
Hélas! Tu reconnais des maisons mortuaires
Que dénoncent, jusqu'à l'obit, parmi la brume,
Ce cérémonial d'une antique coutume:
Un nœud de crêpe noir qui flotte sur les portes;
On dirait des oiseaux cloués, des ailes mortes...
Puis, sur les volets clos, une grande lanterne
Pend, de qui la lueur si grelottante et terne
Brûle, en forme de cœur, dans la prison du verre.
C'est comme de la vie encor qui persévère
Et l'on croirait que l'âme ancienne est là qui pleure
Et guette pour rentrer un peu dans sa demeure!

XXIII

My dream makes a return in peaceful memories
towards your humility, ancient small towns,
towns of my past, elegiac towns
so forlorn, on Christmas and Easter evenings,
towns with names so soft: Audenarde, Malines,
and pious, like praying Ursulines,
their Ave in rhythm with the mournful carillon.
Oh, convent towns, catechist towns,
wax and incense, their sacred scent,
drowsing towns, made gentle martyrs
for not having been loved enough,
who give off the grey dying of their smoke
like a soul's exhausted and virgin lament,
in their death throes in the fog that devours them.

Soft sleepiness of my native towns
which, at evening, I walk again in my mind,
but all along the old quays, my dream, where you wander,
alas! You recognise the funereal mansions
that betray, until memorial amid the mist,
this ceremony of ancient practice:
A black crepe bow that floats on the doors;
with dead wings like a nailed bird…
Then on the fastened shutters, a great lamp
hangs, from which a dull shivering light
burns, heart-shaped, in a prison of glass.
It's as though life here still persists
and you'd think the ancient soul were there which weeps,
watches and waits, to re-enter a while its dwelling place.

XXIV

En province, dans la langueur matutinale
Tinte le carillon, tinte dans la douceur
De l'aube qui regarde avec des yeux de sœur,
Tinte le carillon, – et sa musique pâle
S'effeuille fleur à fleur sur les toits d'alentour,
Et sur les escaliers des pignons noirs s'effeuille
Comme un bouquet de sons mouillés que le vent cueille:
Musique du matin qui tombe de la tour,
Qui tombe de très loin en guirlandes fanées,
Qui tombe de naguère en invisibles lis,
En pétales si lents, si froids et si pâlis
Qu'ils semblent s'effeuiller du front mort des années.

XXV

La ville est morte, morte, irréparablement!
D'une lente anémie et d'un secret tourment,
Est morte jour à jour de l'ennui d'être seule…
Petite ville éteinte et de l'autre temps qui
Conserve on ne sait quoi de vierge et d'alangui
Et semble encor dormir tandis qu'on l'enlinceule;
Car voici qu'à présent, pour embaumer sa mort,
Les canaux, pareils à des étoffes tramées
Dont les points d'or du gaz ont faufilé le bord,
Et le frêle tissu des flottantes fumées
S'enroulent en formant des bandelettes d'eau
Et de brouillard, autour de la pâle endormie
– Tel le cadavre emmailloté d'une momie
Et la lune à son front ajoute un clair bandeau!

XXIV

In the provinces through morning's listlessness
the carillon chimes, chimes in the tenderness
of a dawn that looks on with the eyes of a sister,
the carillon chimes, – and its pale music
is shed bloom by bloom on roofs all around,
and over darkened gable steps
like a bouquet of damp sounds the wind plucks;
music of morning that falls from the tower,
falls from the distance in faded wreaths,
falls from the past in invisible lilies,
in petals so languid, so cold and pale
they seem as if shed from time's dead brow.

XXV

The town is dead, dead, irrevocably!
With a gradual anaemia and secret torment,
died, day by day with the boredom of being alone…
Little lifeless town of another age that preserves
who knows what of the virginal and listless
who seems still to sleep while being enshrouded;
for here now, to embalm her death
are the canals, like woven cloth
whose golden stitch of gaslights have threaded the bank,
and the delicate fabric of drifting smoke
coils up to form strips of water
and mist, about the pale sleeper
– so like a mummy the corpse is enfolded –
and to her brow the moon adds a bright bandage.

AQUARIUM MENTAL

I

L'eau sage s'est enclose en des cloisons de verre
D'où le monde lui soit plus vague et plus lointain;
Elle est tiède, et nul vent glacial ne l'aère;
Rien d'autre ne se mire en ces miroirs sans tain
Où, seule, elle se fait l'effet d'être plus vaste
Et de se prolonger soi-même à l'infini!
D'être recluse, elle s'épure, devient chaste,
Et son sort à celui du verre s'est uni,
Pour n'être ainsi qu'un seul sommeil moiré de rêves!
Eau de l'aquarium, nuit glauque, clair-obscur,
Où passe la pensée en apparences brèves
Comme les ombres d'un grand arbre sur un mur.
Tout est songe, tout est solitude et silence
Parmi l'aquarium, pur d'avoir renoncé,
Et même le soleil, de son dur coup de lance,
Ne fait plus de blessure à son cristal foncé.
L'eau désormais est toute au jeu des poissons calmes
Éventant son repos de leurs muettes palmes;
L'eau désormais est toute aux pensifs végétaux,
Dont l'essor, volontiers captif, se ramifie,
Qui, la brodant comme de rêves, sont sa vie
Intérieure, et sont ses canevas mentaux.
Et, riche ainsi pour s'être enclose, l'eau s'écoute
À travers les poissons et les herbages verts;
Elle est fermée au monde et se possède toute
Et nul vent ne détruit son fragile univers.

MENTAL AQUARIUM

I

The wise water has enclosed herself in partitions of glass
from where the world might be more distant and obscure;
she is lukewarm, and no glacial wind ruffles her;
nothing else reflects in these one-way mirrors
where, alone, she imagines herself spreading further
and extending into the infinite.
Being reclusive, she purges herself, becomes chaste,
and her fate is merged with that of the glass,
to be only a single sleep patterned by dreams.
Aquarium water, drear night, half-light,
where thought passes in brief appearances
like shadows of a great tree over a wall.
All is dream, all is silence and solitude
within the aquarium, pure with renunciation,
and even the sun, with its cruel lance blow,
leaves no further wound in her dark crystal.
Water now left to the play of fish so calm
fanning her rest with their silent palms;
water now left to musing plants,
which blooming, willingly captive, branch out,
which, embroidering her like dreams, are
her interior life, and her mental lacework.
Rich for being enclosed, the water hearkens to herself
through the fish and green pastures;
she is closed to the world and entirely self-possessed
and no wind destroys her fragile universe.

IX

L'aquarium d'abord ne semble pas vivant,
Inhabité comme un miroir dans un couvent;
Crépuscule où toujours se reforme une brume;
Il dort si pâlement qu'on le croirait posthume
Et que les reflets noirs qui viennent et s'en vont
Ne sont qu'ombres sans but sur un lit mortuaire
Et jeux furtifs de veilleuse sur le plafond.

Pourtant dans l'eau, de temps en temps, quelque chose erre,
Circule, se déplie, ou bouge obliquement;
Des frissons lumineux crispent cette eau qui mue,
– Tels les spasmes de lumière du diamant! –
Un poisson sombre ondule, une herbe en deuil remue;
Le sable mou du fond s'éboule comme si
C'était le sablier bouleversé de l'Heure;
Et quelquefois aussi, sur le cristal transi,
Un monstre flasque, en trouble imagerie, affleure,
Cependant que l'eau souffre, en paraissant dormir,
Et sent passer, dans sa morose léthargie,
Mille ombres dont elle ne cesse de frémir
Qui font de sa surface une plaie élargie!

Or n'est-ce pas l'image du sommeil humain
Où, dans l'eau du cerveau qu'on croit vidée et nue,
Des rêves sous-marins sont sans cesse en chemin,

IX

At first the aquarium seems not to be alive,
uninhabited like a mirror in a béguinage;
twilight where a mist always reforms;
so palely it sleeps you would think it posthumous
and that the dark reflections which come and go
were but aimless shadows on a mortuary pillow
and upon the ceiling, the vigil candles' furtive play.

Yet in the water, from time to time, something strays,
circles, opens out or obliquely shifts;
luminous shivers tense this water that drifts
– like spasms of light from a diamond ! –
a murky fish undulates, a weed in mourning stirs,
the soft sand scree of the bed collapses as if
sand in time's hourglass upended;
and sometimes too, on the transfixed crystal,
a flaccid monster, blurred image, shows on the surface,
while the water suffers, seeming to drowse,
and senses, in her morose lethargy, a thousand shadows
giving her ceaseless shivers as they pass
making her surface one great spreading wound.

Now, is this not the image of human sleep
where, in the brain's water one thinks naked and bare,
underwater dreams are ceaselessly voyaging,
Ah! this buried life, never ending...

LE SOIR DANS LES VITRES

XI

Les vitres tout à l'heure étaient pâles et nues.
Mais peu à peu le soir entra dans la maison;
On y sent à présent le péril d'un poison.
C'est que les vitres, pour le soir, sont des cornues
Où se distille on ne sait quoi dans leur cristal;
Le couchant y répand un or qui les colore;
Et pour qu'enfin le crépuscule s'élabore,
L'ombre, comme pour un apprêt médicinal,
Semble y verser ses ténèbres, d'une fiole.
Dans les verres, teintés de ce qui souffre en eux,
Un nuage s'achève, un reflet s'étiole;
Il en germe quelque chose de vénéneux,
Menaçant la maison déjà presque endormie;
Et c'est de plus en plus le nocturne élixir…
Ah! les vitres et leur délétère chimie
Qui chaque soir ainsi me font un peu mourir!

EVENING IN THE WINDOWS

XI

The windows earlier on were pale and stark.
But little by little evening entered the house;
and you sense there now the peril of a poison.
The windows, at evening, are receptacles
where who knows what is distilled in their crystal;
sunset scatters there a gold that colours them;
so that the twilight might at last refine itself,
and shadow, as if for a dose of medicine,
seems to pour darkness there, from a phial.
In the panes, stained with what suffers in them,
a cloud fades away, a reflection dies out;
something poisonous germinates there,
threatening this house on the edge of sleep;
and there's more, and still more, of the nocturnal remedy...
Ah! Those windows and their pernicious chemistry
that each evening makes me die a little more!

LES LIGNES DE LA MAIN

    I

La main s'enorgueillit de sa nudité calme
Et d'être rose et lisse, et de jouer dans l'air
Comme un oiseau narguant l'écume de la mer,
Et de frémir avec des souplesses de palme.

La main exulte; elle est fière comme une rose
— Sans songer que l'envers est un réseau de plis! —
Et fait luire au soleil ses longs ongles polis
Enchâssant dans la chair un peu de corail rose.

La main règne, d'un air impérieux, car tout
Ne s'accomplit que par elle, tout dépend d'elle;
Pour le nid du bonheur, elle est une hirondelle;
Et, pour le vin de joie, elle est le raisin d'août.

La main rit d'être blanche et rose, et qu'elle éclaire
Comme un phare, et qu'elle ait une odeur de sachet;
C'est comme si toujours elle s'endimanchait
À voir les bagues d'or dont se vêt l'annulaire.

Or pendant que la main s'enorgueillit ainsi
D'être belle, et de se convaincre qu'elle embaume,
Les plis mystérieux s'aggravent dans la paume
Et vont commencer d'être un écheveau transi.

Vain orgueil, jeu coquet de la main pavanée
Qui rit de ses bijoux, des ongles fins, des fards;
Cependant qu'en dessous, avec des fils épars,
La Mort tisse déjà sa toile d'araignée.

THE LINES OF THE HAND

    I

The hand prides herself on calm nakedness
and on being rose-hued and smooth, playing in the air
like a bird taunting the ocean's spume,
and on shivering with the palm leaf's suppleness.

The hand exults; she's proud as a rose
– not dreaming the other side is a network of folds! –
and makes her long polished nails shine in the sun
setting in the flesh a little pink coral.

The hand reigns, with an imperious air, for all
is only accomplished by her, all depends on her;
for the nest of happiness, she is a swallow;
and, for the wine of joy, she is the August grape.

The hand laughs, being white and pink, shining out
like a beacon, with her perfumed scent;
it's as if she always wears her Sunday best
to see the gold rings with which the ring finger is dressed.

Now whilst the hand prides herself thus
on her beauty, and to convince herself she's fragrant,
the mysterious folds in the palm worsen
and start to become a paralysing web.

Vain pride, charming game of the prancing hand
who laughs with her jewels, her fine nails, her rouge;
yet, underneath, with fine threads,
Death is already spinning his spider's web!

LES MALADES AUX FENÊTRES

IV

La maladie est si doucement isolante:
Lent repos d'un bateau qui songe au fil d'une eau,
Sans nulle brise, et nul courant qui violente,
Attaché sur le bord par la chaîne et l'anneau.
Avant ce calme octobre, il ne s'appartenait guère:
Toujours du bruit, des violons, des passagers,
Et ses rames brouillant les canaux imagés.
Maintenant il est seul; et doucement s'éclaire
D'un mirage de ciel qui n'est plus partiel;
Il se ceint de reflets puisqu'il est immobile;
Il est libre vraiment puisqu'il est inutile;
Et, délivré du monde, il s'encadre de ciel.

*

'Les maladies des pierres sont des végétations.'
Novalis

*

Quand la pierre est malade elle est toute couverte
De mousses, de lichens, d'une vie humble et verte;
La pierre n'est plus pierre; elle vit; on dirait
Que s'éveille dans elle un projet de forêt,
Et que, d'être malade, elle s'accroît d'un règne,
La maladie étant un état sublimé,
Un avatar obscur où le mieux a germé!
Exemple clair qui sur nous-mêmes nous renseigne:
Si les plantes ne sont que d'anciens cailloux morts
Dont naquit tout à coup une occulte semence,
Les malades que nous sommes seraient alors
Des hommes déjà morts en qui le dieu commence!

INVALIDS AT THE WINDOWS

IV

Sickness is so softly insulating:
slow rest of a boat that dreams, on the water's flow
no breeze, and no current to assault it,
bound to the bank by chain and ring.
Before this calm October, it barely belonged to itself,
always noise, violins, passengers,
and its oars confused the reflected waters.
Now it's alone; and softly lit
by a mirage of the sky no longer partial,
encloses itself with reflections, immobile;
now, unneeded, it's truly free;
and, framed by sky, relieved of the world.

*

'The maladies of stones are vegetation.'
Novalis

*

When the stone is sick it is all covered
with moss, lichens, a life humble and green;
the stone is no longer stone; it lives; you could say
that awakening there is a vision of forests,
and that, being ill, its influence grows,
malady being an exalted state,
dark reincarnation where the best has germinated.
Lucid example which tells us of ourselves:
if the plants are only old dead pebbles
from which suddenly is born an occult seed,
the invalids we are would be then
dead men already, in whom god begins!

XII

L'eau des anciens canaux est débile et malade,
Si morne, parmi les villes mortes, aux quais
Parés d'arbres et de pignons en enfilade
Qui sont, dans cette eau pauvre, à peine décalqués;
Eau vieillie et sans force; eau malingre et déprise
De tout élan pour se raidir contre la brise
Qui lui creuse trop de rides...
Oh! la triste eau
Qui va pleurer sous les ponts noirs et qui s'afflige
Des reflets qu'elle doit porter, eau vraiment lige,
Et qui lui sont comme un immobile fardeau.
Mais, trop âgée, à la surface qui se moire,
Elle perd ses reflets, comme on perd la mémoire,
Et les délaie en de confus mirages gris.
Eau si dolente, au point qu'elle en semble mortelle,
Pourquoi si nue et si déjà nulle?
Et qu'a-t-elle,
Toute à sa somnolence, à ses songes aigris,
Pour n'être ainsi plus qu'un traître miroir de givre
Où la lune elle-même a de la peine à vivre?

XIII (EXTRAIT)

Le malade, quand vient la tristesse nocturne,
Est sensible comme une cendre dans une urne.

Il écoute, et perçoit dans l'air le moindre bruit:
Frisson d'arbre, pas d'un passant, plainte de cloche;
Vigie exacte de tout bruit, il se raccroche
À ces vagues rumeurs dont s'image la nuit
Et par qui le silence apparaît plus immense;
Ce sont les bruits qui font la preuve du silence,
Tandis que les reflets font la preuve de l'eau.
Puis il regarde, et voit des lueurs inconnues:

XII

The waters of the old canals are sick and enfeebled,
so mournful, among the dead towns, along the quays
trimmed by trees and gables in rows, which
in this impoverished water barely show;
aged waters lacking fortitude; sickly, deprived
of all impulsion to steel themselves against the breeze
that furrows them with too many ripples...
Oh sad waters that go to weep
beneath black bridges and are afflicted,
these waters obliged to bear reflections, truly enslaved
to what seems an unyielding burden.
But so ancient, that on the shimmering surface
they lose the reflections, as one might lose a memory,
and spin them out in confusions of grey mirages.
Waters so grief-stricken, they seem about to give in,
why so naked and already of nothing?
What troubles them,
lost in their slumber and embittered dreams,
now nothing more than a deceitful frosted mirror
where the moon herself can barely endure?

XIII (EXCERPT)

The sick man, when nocturnal sadness comes,
is sensitive like ashes in an urn.

He listens, and perceives in the air the least sound:
Shiver of a tree, step of a passer-by, a bell's plaint;
acute vigilante of all sounds, he clings to
these vague murmurs that embellish night
and through which the silence seems more immense;
these sounds reveal the silence,
as water is revealed by reflections.
Then he looks, and sees unknown glimmerings:

Lumières qu'on dirait la fuite d'un flambeau;
Rayon brusque par qui les glaces semblent nues;
Étincelles qui s'en viennent on ne sait d'où;
Or sorti d'un bouquet, projeté d'un bijou;
Phosphorescence de l'ombre ; clarté qui rôde;
Feux follets brefs; scintillement intermittent…
Le malade les suit et son émoi s'en brode.

Mais ces frêles clartés ne durent qu'un instant,
Gouttelettes de couleur qui sont vite bues,
Car c'est d'elles que les ténèbres sont embues;
Le malade pourtant de ses yeux les atteint
– Papillons épinglés à travers la nuit noire –
Et fixe ces lueurs au vol trop vite éteint
Sous le verre silencieux de sa mémoire.

Lights you might say were the flight of a flame;
sudden beam by which the mirrors seem naked;
sparks that come from who knows where;
gold from a bouquet, shot from a jewel,
phosphorescence of shadow; light that prowls;
brief will-o'-the-wisps; intermittent sparkling…
the sick man follows and they sequin his disquiet.

But these frail lights last only a moment,
droplets of colour that are quickly drunk,
for it's these that saturate the darkness;
yet the sick man reaches them with his eyes
– butterflies pinned on the black night –
and fixes these lights, flight extinguished too quickly
beneath the silent glass of his memory.

POUR LA GLOIRE DE MALLARMÉ

C'est tout mystère et tout secret et toutes portes
S'ouvrant un peu sur un commencement de soir;
La goutte de soleil dans un diamant noir;
Et l'éclair vif qu'ont les bijoux des reines mortes.

Une forêt de mâts disant la mer ; des hampes
Attestant des drapeaux qui n'auront pas été;
Rien qu'une rose pour suggérer des roses thé;
Et des jets d'eau soudain baissés, comme des lampes!

Poème! Une relique est dans le reliquaire,
Invisible et pourtant sensible sous le verre
Où les yeux des croyants se sont unis en elle.

Poème! Une clarté qui, de soi-même avare,
Scintille, intermittente afin d'être éternelle;
Et c'est, dans de la nuit, les feux tournants d'un phare!

FOR THE GLORY OF MALLARMÉ

It's all mystery, all secret and all doors
opening a little on to early evening;
drop of sun in a black diamond;
and the vivid glint in the jewels of dead queens.

A forest of masts telling of the sea; flagpoles
vouch for flags that will not have been;
nothing to suggest tea roses but hue of a rose;
and like lamps, fountains abruptly lowered.

Poem! A relic is in the reliquary,
invisible and yet responsive under the glass
where the eyes of believers have united in her.

Poem! A light which, sparing of itself,
sparkles, intermittent that it might be eternal;
and is, in the darkness, a lighthouse's lamps, revolving.

LES FEMMES EN MANTES

    X

Des mantes ont passé dans le vide des rues
Oscillant comme des cloches parmi le soir;
On aurait dit, au loin, des cloches de drap noir
Tintant aussi des glas, et peu à peu décrues...

Des cloches ont tinté, graves d'être pareilles
Aux mantes, et d'aller selon un rythme égal;
On aurait presque dit d'autres petites vieilles
Qui cheminaient dans l'air en robes de métal.

THE WOMEN IN MANTLES

x

Mantles passed by in the void of the streets
swaying like bells amid the evening,
you would think them, at a distance, bells of black cloth
chiming the death knell too, and little by little dying out…

The bells chimed, low pitched to be the same
as the mantles, and to move with the same rhythm;
you might almost have thought other little old women
were wending their way through the air in dresses of metal.

LES RÉVERBÈRES

V

La Nuit est seule, comme un pauvre.
Les réverbères offrent
Leur flamme jaune
Comme une aumône.

La Nuit se tait comme une église close.
Les réverbères mélancoliques
Ouvrent leur flamme rose
Comme des bouquets de lumière,
Des bouquets sous un verre et qui sont des reliques,
Par qui la Nuit s'emplit d'Indulgences plénières.

La Nuit souffre!
Les réverbères en chœur
Dardent leur flamme rouge et soufre
Comme des ex-votos,
Comme des Sacré-Cœur,
Que le vent fait saigner avec ses froids couteaux.

La Nuit s'exalte.
Les réverbères à la file
Déploient leur flamme bleue,
Dans les banlieues,
Comme des âmes qui font halte,
Les âmes en chemin des morts de la journée
Qui rêvent de rentrer dans leur maison fermée
Et s'attardent longtemps aux portes de la ville.

THE STREET LAMPS

    V

Night is alone, like a poor man.
The street lamps offer up
their yellow flame
like alms.

The night keeps silent like a closed church.
The melancholy street lamps
open their pink flame
like bouquets of light,
bouquets beneath a glass, relics,
through which the night fills with plenary indulgences.

Night suffers!
The street lamps in chorus
beam their red flame and sulphur
like votives,
like the sacred hearts
the wind makes bleed with her cold knives.

The night becomes exalted.
The street lamps in single file
unfurl their blue flame
in the suburbs,
like souls which have paused on their journey,
souls of those who died that day,
who dream of returning to their closed house
and linger long at the gates of the town.

VI

La Nuit s'acharne au réverbère qui la nie.

Tout s'endort; seul son feu,
Obstiné comme l'insomnie,
S'attarde, avec son pouls fiévreux,
Ce battement de flamme chaude
Et comme artériel
Qui continuera jusqu'à l'aube.

Le réverbère est seul sous le grand ciel.
Et il voit que, là-bas,
D'autres feux tremblent,
Étoiles qui jamais ne se rassemblent,
Seules comme lui
Dans un éternel célibat.

Ô étoiles, ses sœurs, qu'il nomme dans la nuit!
Un même mal les agite;
Elles sont si tristes;
Elles ont le même sort,
Le même tremblement de fanaux dans un port
À des vaisseaux qui jamais ne partent;
Elles ont la même palpitation,
Les mêmes pulsations,
Comme si un seul cœur, elles et lui, les faisait battre.

Le réverbère songe: «Elles sont comme lui;
Il est comme elles;
Solitude! Et n'avoir à vivre que la nuit!»

Ah! s'éteindre, s'éteindre en une Aube éternelle!

VI

Night hounds the street lamp that negates it.

All falls into slumber; only its fire
stubborn as insomnia,
lingers on, with its feverish pulse,
this fluttering of hot flame
and like an artery
that will endure until dawn.

The street lamp is alone beneath the vast sky;
and sees that, over there,
other lights quiver,
stars that never gather together,
alone like itself
in an eternal celibacy.

Oh stars, its sisters, it names in the night!
The same malady troubles them;
they are so downcast;
they share the same fate,
the same quivering of the port's navigation lights
for vessels that do not depart;
they have the same palpitation,
the same pulse,
as if their beat were made by a single heart.

The street lamp dreams: "They are like it;
and it is like them;
Solitude! And to live only at night!"

Ah, to die out, to die out in an eternal dawn.

LES CYGNES

VI

Les cygnes dans le soir ont soudain déplié
Leurs ailes, parmi l'eau qu'un clair de lune moire;
On y sent se lever un frisson qui va croître,
Comme le long du feuillage des peupliers.

Frisson pareil à ceux d'un grand vent dans les arbres;
C'est comme une musique, en pleurs d'être charnelle;
Musique d'une harpe qui serait une aile,
Car les ailes de cygne ont la forme des harpes.

Ces harpes tout à coup ont déchiré la brume;
Les nénuphars lèvent leurs voiles de béguines;
Tout se recueille; tout écoute les beaux cygnes
Qui dressent sur l'eau morte un arpège de plumes.

Concert nocturne où, seul, je m'arrête de vivre!
Ah! ces harpes de la musique du silence
Dont on ne sait si elle est morte ou recommence;
Et mon cœur s'est gelé dans ces harpes de givre.

THE SWANS

VI

In the evening the swans have suddenly unfolded
their wings, amidst waters the moonlight makes shimmer;
there you sense a wakening shiver which will grow,
as quivering leaves along the poplar rows.

A shiver like that of a great wind in the trees;
like a music, weeping to be made flesh;
music of a harp that would be a wing
for the swans' wings have the shape of harps.

Of a sudden they rent the mist, these harps;
water lilies raise their béguines' shroud,
all draws itself in; all hearkens to the handsome swans
who build a feathered arpeggio on the dead canal.

Nocturnal concert where, alone, I cease to live!
Ah, these harps with the music of silence
dead or starting anew, none can know;
and in these harps of frost my heart has frozen.

Rodenbach the dandy

BIOGRAPHICAL NOTES

GEORGES RODENBACH (1855-1898) was born in Tournai, Belgium but spent his early years in the Flemish city of Ghent and later lived in Paris, where, like his childhood friend and compatriot Emile Verhaeren, he rubbed shoulders with all the main players of the French symbolist movement. Rodenbach's name is forever associated with Bruges, the location for his most celebrated and enduring work, the poetic novel *Bruges-la-Morte* (1892). He also wrote a number of collections of poetry of which *Le Règne du Silence* from 1891 in many ways prefigures *Bruges-la-Morte*. A further novel *Le Carilloneur* (1897) is also set in Bruges. Several books of short stories, prose poems, and a range of essays on such diverse figures as Rodin, Monet, Huysmans, Verlaine and Mallarmé attest to a prodigious literary talent.

Rodenbach was a typical writer of the decadent period, unfailingly anti-bourgeois, solitary, an aesthete suffering some undisclosed malady of the spirit, the victim of a palpable sense of ennui or 'spleen'. But despite his intractable suspicion of modernity and its apparent inherent dangers to artistic integrity, his poetry, like that of Verhaeren, has relevance to our time – unlike many of his peers, whose work now seems enmeshed in the literary frivolities and indulgences of the period. It is no surprise that after his death Rodenbach's precise, poignant, delicate yet existentially muscular poems attracted the likes of Rilke and Proust. These two exceptional diviners of the unacknowledged life secreted within objects and atmospheres saw in them a fellow explorer, a wholly authentic and uncompromising voice, that articulated an interior landscape of the soul like no other. It is this voice that Anglophone readers today can now access after decades of inexplicable neglect.

WILL STONE, born 1966, is a poet, essayist and literary translator who divides his time between Suffolk, North Devon and the European continent. His first poetry collection *Glaciation* (Salt, 2007), won the international Glen Dimplex Award for poetry in 2008. A second collection *Drawing in Ash* was published by Salt in May 2011. Shearsman Books republished the two Salt collections in new editions in August 2015 and published a third collection *The Sleepwalkers* in April 2016 to critical acclaim.

Will's published translations include *Les Chimères* by Gérard de Nerval (Menard, 1999), *To The Silenced – Selected Poems of Georg Trakl* (Arc Publications, 2005) and *Poems* by Emile Verhaeren (Arc Publications, 2013). *Journeys*, a first English translation of Stefan Zweig's European travel essays, was published by Hesperus Press in 2010. This was followed by *Rilke in Paris* by Maurice Betz (Hesperus, 2012) which also included a translation of Rilke's *Notes on the Melody of Things*. Hesperus published two more translations, *Nietzsche* by Stefan Zweig (2013) and *On the End of the World* by Joseph Roth (2013), collecting hitherto unknown essays from his Parisian exile during the 1930s. Pushkin Press published a first English translation of *Montaigne* by Stefan Zweig (2015) and then *Messages from a Lost World* (2016), Zweig's essays and speeches from the 1930s. Pushkin will publish a further collection of Zweig's essay portraits on his contemporaries as *Encounters and Destinies – A Farewell to Europe* in 2017. Hesperus Press will publish a translation of *Friedrich Hölderlin – Life, Poetry and Madness* by Wilhelm Waiblinger also in 2017. A *Collected Poems of Georg Trakl* will appear from Seagull Books in spring 2018.

Will is currently writing a prose work on the more overlooked elements of the cultural history and landscape of Belgium. He also plans to write the first monograph in English on the overlooked Belgian painter Léon Spilliaert. Further translation projects include a first English translation of *Poems to Night* by Rilke. Will contributes essays and reviews of art and literature to, amongst others, *The TLS*, *The London Magazine*, *Poetry Review*, *Apollo Magazine*, *The Burlington Magazine* and *The White Review*.